VALENTINE SIMMES

Printer to Drayton, Shakespeare, Chapman, Greene,

Dekker, Middleton, Daniel, Jonson, Marlowe,

Marston, Heywood, and other Elizabethans

By

W. CRAIG FERGUSON

Charlottesville, Virginia

Bibliographical Society of the University of Virginia

1968

C

Preface

This study was originally the main part of a dissertation presented to the University of Birmingham. During the last few years I have followed up some of the loose ends, and have slightly altered some sections as new information has come my way. Some sections are already inadequate, as new techniques, such as the use of beta-radiography to record watermarks, have become known, or where the earlier publication of part of this study has led to advances upon it. These shortcomings will be noted in the text.

It was Mr John Cook Wyllie who first suggested to me the need for detailed study of individual printers, and who pointed out Simmes as a possible starter. I am very much in his debt for his interest and enthusiasm during the years that have elapsed since he made the suggestion. The work was done at the Shakespeare Institute under the general supervision of Professor Allardyce Nicoll, and more particularly Messrs J. R. Brown, R. H. Hosley, and J. K. Walton. To all of them I am indebted. Because the Institute was a small, closely-knit structure, I, like all who worked there, owe much to all the Fellows and staff, and to my fellow students.

Bibliographers are always beholden to librarians, and I would like to record my appreciation for the unfailing courtesy and help I received from the staffs of the British Museum, the Bodleian, the Cambridge University Library, the Shakespeare Birthplace Trust, and the Henry E. Huntington Library. I owe a special debt to Miss Maria Dubno, the Shakespeare Institute Librarian, who was always willing to assist perplexed students.

The Canada Council provided a travel grant which allowed me to visit the Huntington Library to study the *Malcontent* quartos; I wish to thank the Council for its assistance. The photographs of ornaments are reproduced through the courtesy of the Huntington, Folger, and Bodleian libraries.

Kingston, Ontario
January 11, 1967   W. C. F.

Contents

Preface iii

I   Biography 5

II   Business History 11

III   The Compositors of *Henry IV, Part 2, Much Ado About Nothing.*
      The Shoemakers' Holiday, and *The First Part of the*
      Contention 27

IV   Type-Founts, Ornaments, and Paper

     1. Type-Founts 39

     2. Devices and Compartments 43

     3. Ornamental Pieces 45

     4. Factotums 54

     5. Decorative Initials 60

     6. Paper 64

V   Some Bibliographical Problems

     1. Layout 79

     2. Printers' Measures 83

     3. Proof Corrections 84

     4. Errata Lists 85

     5. Shared Printing 86

     6. The Third Preface to *Mæoniæ* 89

     7. The Third Quarto of *Hamlet* 90

     8. Authors and Dedicatees 90

     9. The *Malcontent* Quartos, 1604 94

Bibliography 103

Index 110

Chapter I

Biography

The only record of the birth and parentage of Valentine Simmes is in the Stationers' Register entry of his apprenticeship to Henry Sutton in 1577. He is stated there to be "sonne of Richard Symmes of Adderbury in the county of Oxford Sher[e]man."[1] He must have been born before 1561, as he received his freedom in 1585, and the earliest age at which one could become free was twenty-four.[2]

Valentine Simmes was apprenticed to Henry Sutton, an older Stationer who was still taking apprentices although he had ceased printing some fifteen years before Simmes came under him.[3] Sutton died before Simmes finished his apprenticeship, and Simmes was presented for his freedom by Sutton's widow, Johane.[4] According to the terms of Simmes's apprenticeship contract, he should have become free at Christmas, 1584. Perhaps one reason his freedom was held up until March was that he had not yet reached his 24th birthday.

At some time during his apprenticeship Simmes worked under Henry Bynneman; indeed, he may have spent most of his time in Bynneman's shop, for he was trained as a compositor, training he would be unlikely to receive at this time in Sutton's shop. Certainly Simmes was in Bynneman's shop early in his apprenticeship, as Bynneman died in 1583.[5] Several years later, in 1596, Simmes was able to obtain some of Bynneman's 'copies' on the grounds that he had at one time been servant to the older stationer.[6] It is interesting to note in passing that Nicholas Ling was apprenticed to Bynneman from September 1570 to January 1579.[7] He and Simmes had frequent business dealings later, and it is probable that they met and worked together in Bynneman's shop.

1. Arber, E.: *A Transcript of the Registers of the Company of Stationers of London: 1554-1640 A.D.* (1950) II, 74. Hereafter referred to as Arber.

2. For further discussion, see Blagden, C.: *The Stationers' Company* (1960), p. 35.

3. According to Paul G. Morrison's *Index of Printers, Publishers and Booksellers in STC* (1950), Sutton printed his last five books in 1562.

4. Arber, II, 694.

5. Arber, II, 121.

6. Greg, W. W. and E. Boswell: *Records of the Court of the Stationers' Company 1576-1602—from Register B.* (1930) pp. lxxvi and 53.

7. Arber, I, 434 and II, 679.

On March 8, 1585, Simmes was admitted a freeman of the Station-ers' Company. Nothing further is heard of him until July, 1589, when he was hired by John Hodgkins for the decidedly dangerous job of helping print some secret pamphlets for the 'second Marprelate' press.

Our main source of information about Simmes's movements at this time comes from his examination on December 10 of the same year,[8] when, it is believed, the rack was used to extract information. Accord-ing to Simmes's deposition, Hodgkins hired him and another printer, Arthur Thomlyn, to print accidences, which were, incidentally, privi-leged. Hodgkins promised Simmes £20 a year with meat and drink, and promised Thomlyn £8 together with his sustenance.

Simmes left almost immediately for the country, visiting his father at Adderbury on the way. He met the other conspirators at Warwick, and they proceeded to Wolston Priory, near Coventry, where they printed two pamphlets, *Theses Martinianae* (STC 17457) and *The Just Censure and Reproof* (STC 17458). We can assume that Simmes knew by this time, if he had not known from the beginning, that he had not been hired for the printing of accidences! The conspirators then moved their portable press to Newton Lane near Manchester, but through an accident they were discovered, and arrested as they were printing still another pamphlet.

Simmes, Thomlyn, and Hodgkins were examined by the Earl of Derby who, realizing the importance of the catch, sent them immedi-ately to London. Here they were examined before the Privy Council and kept prisoners until December. Simmes was last heard of in the affair on December 10, the day his last statement was taken. It is not known when he was released.

In 1594 appeared the first books bearing Simmes's imprint, and it may be assumed that it was in this year that he began his career as a printer and bookseller. He may have taken Richard Cowper as an apprentice in March of this year,[9] and certainly on September 30 he took John Bodley as his apprentice.[10] The next year we learn where Simmes had set up his business, as the title-page of *The Government*

8. Included in Appendix 'C' of Pierce, W.: *An Historical Introduction to the Marpre-late Tracts.* (1908). The following discus-sion is based on Pierce's account, backed up by references to the depositions.

9. Arber II, 214. The entry is under date of December 6, 1596, but a marginal note reads "March 1594." If Simmes did take Cowper, he did not have him for long, for on March 26, 1595, Cowper became appren-ticed to Richard Jones (II, 202), and the only hint that he had ever served with Simmes came on January 17, 1599, when Cowper was transferred from Jones to William Whyte, with the consent of Simmes, "with whom he hath served." (II, 233)

10. Arber II, 197.

of Health (STC 4042) advertises his place of business in considerable detail and large type as "dwelling in adling street, at the signe of the white Swan, neare Bainards Castel."

From 1594 until 1622 we find Simmes's name cropping up here and there in the Stationers' records, sometimes in connection with the entry of books, sometimes because he was in trouble with his peers, and it is through these entries that we can follow his career.

In 1595 came his first brush with the Company when he printed the *Grammar and Accidence* (shades of '89!) which was the privilege of Francis Flower. According to one register entry on July 15 (the end of the Wardens' year), his press had been carried to the hall in punishment,[1] and according to another entry on the same day, about twenty reams of Simmes's paper remained at the hall.[2] The account of the incident in the Court Book under September 27 mentions neither paper nor press, but speaks instead of "certen fourmes of letters and other printinge stuffe" and orders the letters "molten accordinge to the said decree and soe with the reste of the said printinge stuffe Rede-liuered vnto the said Valentyne."[3]

Another entry in the Court Book, on June 7, 1596, notes that Simmes and another printer, Robert Baines, "have putt ou' their twoo apprentices to Iames Robert" and orders them not to take any more apprentices until these have finished their time.[4]

Over the next few years came a number of small infractions. In September, 1598, he paid a small fine "for printing a thing disorderly."[5] He was one of the fourteen printers warned by the Company upon receipt of the commandments from Archbishop Whitgift and Bishop Bancroft on June 1, 1599.[6] In October he had some "printed papers

1. Arber I, 578.

2. Arber I, 581. MEMORANDUM there remayne in the hall certen leaves [i.e. printed sheets] of th[e] *accidence* amountinge to aboute xx Reames which were siesed in th[e h]andes of valentyne Symmes.

3. Greg & Boswell, p. 52. Blagden suggests that this may not have been regarded, unofficially at least, as too great a crime, for he says, on p. 44, that ". . . it was sporting to print the copy of a monopolist, just as today some people consider it sporting to swindle the Treasury or a nationalized undertaking."

4. Greg & Boswell, p. 55. If the Simmes

apprentice was John Bodley, this would mean that Simmes should have no more apprentices until May 3, 1602, when Bodley was made free (Arber II, 732). However, he took another apprentice on October 5, 1601 (Arber II, 257), and Bodley, when his time came, was presented by Simmes himself. Also, this makes suspect the marginal note on Cowper's apprenticeship record (Arber II, 214). Perhaps Simmes did take Cowper late in 1596, and tried to make it appear that he had had him before the trouble mentioned above.

5. Arber II, 829.

6. Arber III, 677. In the warning it was ordered "That all NASSHes bookes . . . be

Remayning in hall,"[7] and the Master and Wardens are to deal with him about it. This could have been another confiscation similar to that of 1595, although possibly it refers to the confiscation ordered by the ecclesiastical authorities the previous June.

There was no more trouble until August 3, 1601, when Simmes was fined 3/4 "for pryntinge *A proclamation* formerly printed for the Crowne office whiche he hathe nowe this tyme printed without Alowance or entrance."[8] Two months later he was ordered not to reprint Latimer's *Sermons*[9] and to bring "A true accoumpt of the whole Impression that he did print thereof." In addition he was requested to produce his warrant for printing the *Stannary Laws of Devon* (STC 6798) which he had published the previous year. Neither of these transactions implies wrongdoing on Simmes's part, but rather suggests that the Court of the Stationers' Company was keeping a wary eye on him, and making certain he lived up to his obligations. He had printed the Latimer on condition that he "paie vjd in the li to th[e] use of the poore," and now he was being asked to show "What the vjd in the li did come to." Again, he presumably satisfied the Court's concern for the *Stannary Laws* as the matter was not heard of again.

Four days later, on the fifth of October, Simmes entered another apprentice, Charles Crowley.[1] It will be remembered that according to the judgment passed against him in 1595 Simmes was not to take apprentices until his old transferred apprentice had finished his time.

Twice during 1603 Simmes was fined for disorderly printing. On June 7 he was fined 14/6 for printing "a ballad belonginge to mistres Alldee."[2] Six months later he was again in trouble, and ordered to bring in "Thirtie bookes of *the welshbate* [STC 20170] and all the ballades that he hath printed of *the Traitours lately Arrayned at Winchester*." He was fined the usual 14/6 for unlicensed printing, but in addition a warning was written into the record, telling him "not to meddle with printing or selling any of the same bookes or ballades hereafter."[3]

---

taken wheresoeuer they maye be found and that none of [his] bookes bee euer printed hereafter." Simmes printed *Nashes Lenten Stuffe* (STC 18370) during this year. It had been entered to Burby on January 11, 1601 (III, 134) and presumably printed before June.

7. Greg & Boswell, p. 74.

8. Arber II, 833. Another 'sporting' venture?

9. Greg & Boswell, p. 82. Simmes obtained permission to print the *Sermons* in December, 1594 (Arber II, 667) but there was some doubt as to whether he should print it for "the stock, or generally for the partners, or for the whole companyne that will laye on paper."

1. Arber II, 257.

2. Arber II, 836.

3. Arber III, 249.

A year later, on December 3, 1604, Simmes took another apprentice, William Boseman. There was one more fine, on February 4, 1605,
for breaking order.[4]

Of course, information is continually turning up in unlikely places
as scholars continue to dig into uncatalogued manuscript collections.
One such find was the following, found by an historian cataloguing a
famous collection. It is an unsigned, undated letter, endorsed by the
writer "To the King's most Excellent Majesty," informing us that, at
about this time, Simmes was in serious enough trouble to be impris-
oned. The note reads:

"Most gracious Sovereign. Valentine Symmes who was now taken printing
seditious books, has done the like seven times before this; first he printed
the things of Martin Marprelate, after has been meddling in Popish books,
he by forbearing has become worse.

Henry Oven [Owen?] now prisoner in the Clinck having the liberty of
the prison joined with Symmes. Oven has been more than twenty times for
popish tricks [tractis?] committed.

It is needful that papists committed be kept close prisoners.

Keepers of prisons that go not with their prisoner are unfit & unfaithful
to your Majesty, who knows what such people does.[sic]

If the keeper be punished & displeased [sic] it will make all the rest more
vigilant.[5]"

This is all we know, but it is backed up by the fact that Simmes was
officially replaced as a printer early in 1607.[6]

No books bearing Simmes's imprint can be found for the years 1608
and 1609. During this period his name appears in the Company Poor
Book, first on Good Friday, 1608,[7] when he received five shillings. He
was next heard of on April 19, 1610, when he signed over *The Shoemakers' Holiday* (STC 6523,4) to John Wright with the stipulation
that Simmes should himself print the book "if he haue a printinge
house of his owne."[8] It would appear that Simmes had not been able

---

4. Arber II, 287, 840.

5. The Hatfield Papers. This note was
found by David McN. Lockie, Esq., whose
transcript is quoted. Mr. Lockie felt that
the location of the note pointed to a date
around 1606 to 1608.

6. Jackson, W. A.: *Records of the Court
of the Stationers' Company 1602 to 1640.*
(1957), p. 24. Under date of March 2,

1606/7 we find "Willm Hall ys admitted
to be a printer in the place of Valentine
Symmes." On the other hand, the list of
printers appended to Arber (III, 703) has
the entry, "1608 Henry Ballard from Simmes."

7. When the records begin. There may
have been earlier payments and the records
lost.

8. Arber III, 431.

to re-establish himself, for the edition published by Wright the same
year bears the imprint of George Eld.

Simmes's career as a printer and publisher was now about over.
He had no shop of his own, and was officially prohibited from carrying
on his trade. However, he did manage to put forth five books bearing
his imprint; one book each in 1610 and 1611 were printed for him,
two in 1611 were printed, according to the imprint, by him, and a lone
book in 1612 was printed by Simmes and R. Blower.

Records of payments to Simmes appear again in the Poor Book,
commencing on June 23, 1618, and continuing until September 27,
1623.[9] There are in addition two more references to Simmes in the
Stationers' Register. In 1619 he assigned six books over to Griffen,[1]
and, finally, we find him petitioning the Archbishop for reinstatement
as a master printer. The matter was referred to the Stationers, who
decided that he should not be reinstated. It appears from the entry
that they had been giving him a pension of £4 a year, and that, as
further compensation, they were willing to give him an extra £10 over
the next four or five years, on the compassionate grounds that "he is a
very poore man and a member of the Companie."[2]

9. The late Mr. Cyprian Blagden examined the Poor Book for me; here is his
account of the Simmes payments:

"On the 23rd of June 1618 he was once
again paid 10s. and this payment was
repeated quarter by quarter up to the
20th June 1621. On the 26th September
1621 his pension was increased to 20s. a
quarter and so continued until the 22nd
March 1623. On the 20th June 1623 he was
apparently paid 30s. (an unusual sum and
just conceivably a clerical error). On the
27th September 1623 he was again paid
20s. but the entry appears at the end of
the list of those receiving this amount
instead of, as before, nearer the middle of
the list. It is possible, therefore, that an
extra payment was made to him in June
because of desperate illness and that the
new placing of his name in September may
be due to lack of knowledge whether or
not he were still alive. (These of course are
my own speculations.)"

1. Arber III, 661.

2. Jackson, pp. 380-1 for the ecclesiastical
decision, p. 152 for the Stationers' Court
decision. The Poor Book entry of 30s. on
June 20, 1623, noted by Mr. Blagden, suggests that Simmes took the alternative of
an increased pension, suggested by the
Court, instead of the extra £10.

Chapter II

Business History

In assessing a trade printer's business, it is necessary to arrive at some estimate of the volume of his trade, but it is difficult to determine the amount of labour involved in composing and printing off books. To be truly accurate in determining the work involved in composing, one would have to count every piece of type the compositor placed in his stick. As this is obviously not feasible, another method must be found.

It is possible to count the pages or formes which a shop has produced, but these are inaccurate measures as both pages and formes vary considerably in the amount of work they represent. A more accurate yet readily manageable method of estimating the compositors' labour has been adopted in this study. The linear length of the type set for each book has been calculated by multiplying the length of a representative line of type (in metric measure) by the number of lines or type on a representative page by the number of pages of text in the book. This calculation has given, in a round number of meters, the 'length' of type set up for each book. Take, for example, Latimer's *Sermons* (STC 15281). The lines of type measure 87mm., there are 38 lines of type per page, and there are 659 pages of text. By multiplying these figures together, we find that there are 2178.6 meters of type in this book.

This method is still not completely accurate, for type of different founts will vary considerable in the width of an en, where even a fraction of a millimeter's difference is important when spread over an entire book. Another assumption which leads to some negligible error is that all lines are the full length of the measure, which they are not. These amounts of error, however, may be tolerated. An attempt to cut down error has been made by counting only text-pages, eliminating from the count blank pages, title-pages, and pages of commendatory matter which is often set in a fount of a size different from that of the text or frequently occupies part of a page only. Errata and contents pages were also dropped from the count. The final figures, therefore, will be conservative, but, while they will not show all the work done in the shop, they will provide a reasonably accurate guide to the shop's output of type-setting from year to year.

When the yearly totals are transferred to a graph (figure 1), we can plainly see the fluctuations in Simmes's business. Of course, it must be remembered, here and throughout the study, that all figures and discussion are based on extant books, and our picture of Elizabethan printing must remain forever inaccurate, as it is useless to guess at the number of books which have disappeared.

This method of computing production gives a daily production figure comparable with that suggested by McKerrow. Taking Simmes's busiest year, 1596, as representing a year of full production, we find that the extant books involved setting 8500 meters of type. Assuming a working year of 300 days, this means that, on the average, 28.3 meters of type were set in a day. The average quarto page is 85mm. in width with 35 lines of type to the page, or a fraction under three meters in total length. In an average day, then, about 9½ such pages could have been set. This is just over two formes.

These figures agree fairly closely with McKerrow who suggested that one compositor would be able to set one quarto sheet per day.[1] This would be a very steady rate of composition, which McKerrow arrived at by examining three instances in which the rate of composition had been calculated.

II

The first books bearing Simmes's imprint appeared in 1594. There were four of them, brought to Simmes by five publishers. Gregory Seton, who brought *The Commonwealth of England* (STC 22860), was an older, established publisher, but nothing is known about the Widow Newman, who had Simmes print *The Pattern of Painful Adventures* (STC 709).

The other three publishers who came to Simmes this year were all young men who had recently established themselves in business.[2] Thomas Adams, who had taken his freedom in 1590, gave Simmes his wholehearted support for three years, bringing all his known books to him during the years 1594, 5, and 6.

Two other young men, John Busby and Nicholas Ling, came jointly with a single book, *Matilda* (STC 7206). Busby brought a considerable

---

1. McKerrow, R. B.: "Edward Allde as a typical trade printer." *The Library*, (1929) pp. 142-3.

2. All personal references to Stationers are taken from R. B. McKerrow's *A Dictionary of Printers and Booksellers in England, Scotland and Ireland, and of Foreign Print-* *ers of English books, 1557-1640.* (1910) unless otherwise stated. All references to a printer's or publisher's output are to figures obtained by checking the appropriate references in Morrison. They will, of course, be below the actual output figures, as they do not incorporate additions to STC or books no longer extant.

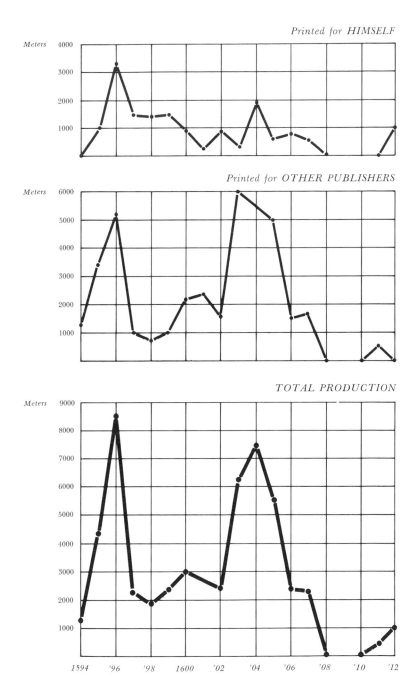

Figure 1: The amount of typesetting (in meters) in Simmes's shop 1594-1612

amount of work to Simmes in the next two years, and Ling became Simmes's most important business associate.[3] We have seen that Simmes and Ling probably met during their apprenticeship.[4] Ling and Busby came to Simmes with what seems to be a most curious assignment. The only extant copy of an 'edition' of Drayton's *Matilda* bears a cancel title-page with Simmes's imprint, but the text is that of a previous edition (STC 7205) which had been printed for Ling and Busby the same year, probably (on the evidence of ornaments) by James Roberts. The two possibilities are that Simmes was, for some reason, actually requested to print a cancel title-page, or, that he did in fact print a second edition of the book, which has not survived, and that, for some reason, a Simmes title-page was used to replace the missing title-page of a Roberts copy.[5]

In 1595 Simmes's output (in linear measure) almost quadrupled over the previous year. Almost half of the year's business was brought by Ralph Jackson, a near contemporary, who had Simmes print two fairly long books by the anti-Catholic writer, Francis Bunny.[6] Jackson, however, brought no more books to Simmes after this year.

Three of the publishers of the previous year, Adams, Busby, and Ling, continued handing over books to Simmes, and he also printed a book each for Richard Boyle, a man noted for his puritan sympathies,[7] and Humphrey Lownes, another of the younger stationers. The book he printed for Lownes, *The Gentleman's Academy* (STC

3. A curious practice has complicated Ling's publications. On over half the books he published, no other name than his own appears on the imprint; if a printer is mentioned at all, it is only by his initials. Very often, too, Ling himself is listed only by his initials. Thus we find that, of the 71 books Ling published, 17 do not name a printer, 30 indicate the printer by initials, and 17 indicate Ling himself by initials. The realization of this practice led to an examination of the 17 Ling books which do not name any printer, and several of these, on the evidence of ornaments and typographical practices, can be assigned to Simmes. Again, it sheds some light upon the publication of Q1 *Hamlet* (STC 22275). The imprint says only "printed for N.L. and John Trundell." The failure to disclose the printer's name can now be seen as normal procedure where Ling was involved as a publisher. The prevalence of these patterns in Ling's books indicates

also that the publisher was responsible in some measure at least for the make-up of his title-pages.

4. See p. 5 above.

5. The present owners of STC 7206, Sion College, know nothing of the volume's past history. The only copy of STC 7205 is in the Huntington Library. It appears, from correspondence, that the watermarks in the texts of the two volumes are identical, and that the title-page of the Huntington copy, while not conjugate with A4, has the same mark.

6. *Survey of the Pope's Supremacy* (STC 4101), *Truth and Falsehood* (STC 4102).

7. He is mentioned in Martin Marprelate's *Just Censure* (STC 17458) as selling puritan literature, including the Marprelate tracts.

3314), was one of the most carefully produced of any of Simmes's books. Lownes did not, to our knowledge, have Simmes print anything else for him.

It was during this year that Simmes printed the first books bearing his name alone on the imprint. Publishing was to remain the smaller part of his business, but was to make up a substantial part of his output nevertheless. One of his first books was medical, Bullein's *Government of Health* (STC 4042), the other a devotional book, Strigelius's *Third proceeding in the harmony of King David's harp* (STC 23361).

Simmes's busiest year was 1596, for in it he appears to have set more type than in any other year of his career, and fully double that of 1595. It is possible that the figures for this year are deceptive, as the single book which made up a quarter of his production, Latimer's *Sermons* (STC 15281), had been assigned to him in December, 1594,[8] and he may have been printing it through 1595, although there is no proof of this.[9] The Stationers' Register informs us that this book was the property of the Company, and was assigned by them to Simmes. Another book which was the property of the Company, Apuleius's *Golden Ass* (STC 720), was assigned to Simmes for printing early in 1596.[1]

Both entries suggest that Simmes petitioned the Company to be allowed to print these books, and both show that Simmes had to fulfill certain obligations for the privilege of printing them. The right to print the *Sermons* was "Graunted vnto him" on condition that he pay into the Company's poor fund, and the *Golden Ass* had not only this condition attached, but also the cautious proviso that he could not print it if it were the property of another member.

It was about this time that Simmes began dabbling in the printing of Catholic books. There is no reason to believe that his interest was other than mercenary, just as it was likely that the wage and not sympathies involved him in the Marprelate printing. One book dated 1596 can be traced to his press. This is *A treatise showing the possibility and conveniency of the real presence of our Saviour in the blessed Sacrament* (STC 24249)[2] which, according to the imprint, was printed

---

8. Arber II, 667.

9. The watermark found on sheet 'a' of the BM copy of the *Sermons* appears to be identical with one of the marks found in Bunny's *Truth and Falsehood*, which Simmes printed in 1595. The presence of the mark (#4 in this study) suggests that

the *Sermons* could have been in progress at much the same time.

1. Arber III, 59.

2. Listed as #925 in *A Catalogue of Catholic Books in English printed abroad or secretly in England 1558-1640* (1956) by A.

at Antwerp by Ioachim Trognesius. It is possible that the first sheet
was printed abroad, containing as it does ornaments Simmes never
used elsewhere, but the remainder of the book was printed with
Simmes's type and contains also one of his initials, listed in a later
chapter as 'A-5'.

Adams again brought all his books to Simmes (with what persua-
sion on Simmes's part we cannot know), and he printed another edition of *The Triumphs over death* (STC 22972) for Ling and Busby.
Clement Knight, who had been recently translated from the Drapers,
brought one book to Simmes, and Bonham Norton brought another.
Knight was to come again a few years later, but Norton, as far as is
known, brought only the one book, and that near the beginning of
his substantial career.

It was during this year that Simmes began in earnest to publish his
own books. Seven books printed this year bear Simmes's name alone on
the imprint, and these account for over a third of his compositors'
setting. He never again published this much material in one year, or so
many titles. Six of his own books were of a theological nature, and
the seventh was a medical book.

For the next three years Simmes's production fell off badly. These
were normal business years in the trade generally (as a glance at a
chronological STC will show) but Simmes's production slumped from
8500 meters in 1596 to 2200 meters in 1597, to 1950 meters in 1598,
and up only slightly in 1599 to almost 2300 meters. The overt reason
for the drop in Simmes's output is fairly obvious: not one of the
publishers whose trade he had built up over the previous three years
returned to him with work. Why they did not use Simmes's press
remains a mystery about which speculation is futile. Nicholas Ling,
who was quite active during these years, gave him no business in
1597, and two of his most reliable publishers, Adams and Busby, never
again to our knowledge brought books to Simmes, although he had
been their principal printer for the previous three years.

Simmes printed only three books for other publishers in 1597. He
printed the *Queen of Navarre's tale* (STC 17323) for John Oxenbridge,
a small publisher who published only the one book that year. Andrew
Wise had Simmes print two plays, relatively short books, but of interest
to us because of their literary importance. These plays were the first
quartos of Shakespeare's *Richard II* (STC 22307) and *Richard III*
(STC 22314).[3] These were the first plays Simmes printed, and show

---

F. Allison and D. M. Rogers. Hereafter   3. But this book was shared. See post
referred to as A & R.   p. 86fn.

the uncluttered appearance and careful craftsmanship which were to mark most of his dramatic work.

Thomas Creede, another important trade printer, was linked with Simmes in an unusual business arrangement, the printing of Le Fevre's *Ancient history of the destruction of Troy* (STC 15379). This book, as we have it in the only extant copy, is divided into three parts, each with a separate title-page. The two printers divided the work more or less evenly between themselves. Creede printed the first half of the book, ending his register at V6v. Both his title-pages are dated 1596. Simmes began printing with a new alphabet in the middle of the second part of the book, apparently with the same stock of paper. His stint included the third title-page, which contains no mention of Creede, and is dated 1597, which suggests that the work was done during the winter of 1596-7. A curious point about the book is that a third printer was involved, and, on coarse paper, printed two leaves which are inserted between 2S8 and 2T2, and another two leaves in Creede's section, between G5 and 6.

Once again Simmes printed a recusant book, *A short treatise of the Sacrament of Penance* (STC 3942)[4] which was sent forth with an imprint bearing only the date, and can be assigned to Simmes's press on the evidence of the type and an initial, his 'W-1'.

The remainder of Simmes's output for 1597 consisted of three books which he published for himself; one devotional book, and the other two, light secular works.

In 1598 Simmes printed even less than he did in 1597. Two publishers who had come to him the previous year, Oxenbridge and Wise, gave him business again this year. Oxenbridge is known to have published two books in 1598, and Simmes printed both of them. Andrew Wise published the second and third editions of *Richard II* (STC 22308,9) and Simmes printed them both. Ling brought only one slight book, Lodge's *Rosalynde* (STC 16667).[5]

Simmes printed one book this year which bears a false imprint, but probably without any intent to deceive. The book, Nicholas Breton's *A solemn passion of the soul's love* (STC 3696) bears the imprint, "Printed by Simon Stafford for William Barley", but the evidence of ornaments and typography gives the book to Simmes. Stafford was just at the beginning of his career, and this is the only book bearing his imprint this year; by 1599 he had his own stock and was in business for himself.

4. A & R #177.

5. I am indebted to Mr. J. C. Wyllie for pointing out this book and the next.

The remainder of Simmes's printing in 1598 was for himself. This part of his work made up the bulk of his total output for the year, and was composed mostly of secular works, with only the short visitation articles being of mild religious interest (STC 10253).

Business increased slightly in 1599, coming up to the meagre level of 1597. Simmes's published work remained at much the same level as the previous year, comprising two volumes, a book of sermons (STC 24003) and a treatise on navigation (STC 26019).

Simmes obtained work from four publishers this year, three of them bringing books for the first time. William Aspley brought a play, *A warning for fair women* (STC 25089). Aspley had begun publishing this same year, and was to publish many plays during his career, bringing several of them to Simmes.

Nicholas Ling came back to Simmes this year with two books: Greene's *Menaphon* (STC 12273) and the delightful *Silkworms and their flies* (STC 17994). He came also with Cuthbert Burby and had Simmes print *Nashes Lenten Stuff* (STC 18370). It was probably for printing this book that Simmes found his name at the bottom of the Archbishop's list that June.[1]

The fourth publisher to give Simmes work this year was another man associated with Ling, and newly established as a Stationer:— Thomas Bushell. Bushell became free early in 1599[2] and that year published two books. Creede printed one of them, and the other, Weever's *Epigrams* (STC 25224), was printed by Simmes.

In 1600 Simmes's business continued to increase modestly. There was a falling-off of his own publishing, but he contracted twice as much work from fellow stationers as he had been able to contract in 1599. The most important customer this year was Thomas Bushell, Ling's former apprentice, who had Simmes print the three books he published in this his second year of business. These three books (STC 3675, 11578, and 20150) made up just over a third of Simmes's production for the year.

Three publishers, all relatively new to the craft, brought books to Simmes this year. Matthew Law, who had not published anything for four years, commissioned Simmes to print the only book he published this year, the no longer extant *Cato Christianus*.[3] Thomas Pavier had transferred to the Stationers' company in 1600, and had begun by publishing five books his first year. One of these books was a play, *Sir John Oldcastle* (STC 18795), and this found its way to Simmes's shop.

---

1. Arber III, 678. See discussion above.   3 Mentioned in Ames, *Typographical Antiquities*, Vol. 2, p.1290.

2. Arber II, 723.

Thomas Millington, another sporadic publisher, brought one book to Simmes. This was his second edition of *The first part of the Contention* (STC 26100), the first edition (STC 26099) having been printed for him in 1594 by Creede. It is interesting to note that Millington published only three plays this year, and took each to a different printer: *Richard Duke of York* (STC 21006a) was taken to William White, *The Contention* to Simmes, and, with Busby as a partner, the first quarto of *Henry V* (STC 22289) was taken to Creede. It does seem odd that Creede did not print the second edition of *The Contention*, having done the first.

By 1600 Simmes had printed several dramatic quartos, and his careful workmanship certainly deserved the custom he received. Two publishers who had previously brought plays to him were Andrew Wise and William Aspley. These men joined in 1600 to publish authorized first quartos of two of Shakespeare's plays, *Much Ado about Nothing* (STC 22304) and *Henry IV, Part II* (STC 22288), and had Simmes print both books. These plays appear to have been considered a single venture, as one title-page was printed in part from the standing type of the other.

Simmes published six books for himself this year, which, in terms of linear measure, made up less than a quarter of his output. Most of them were secular books, and included one interesting play, the first quarto of Dekker's *Shoemakers' Holiday* (STC 6523). There is no Stationers' Register entry for this play, but Simmes probably established his right simply by printing it, for ten years later he made a normal transfer of the play to John Wright.[4]

The following year saw a decline in Simmes's business, caused by a sharp falling-off of his personal publishing. His contracted work continued to rise slightly over the 1600 figures, but not nearly enough to off-set the slump in his own publishing ventures. The most important work Simmes did this year was the printing of the works of Samuel Daniel (STC 6236,7) for Simon Waterson. This book alone made up half of Simmes's printed output for 1601. Some copies of the book bear the variant imprint date of 1602, and were printed on inferior paper. However, they are the same edition, and the variant date may mean only that these copies were machined off late in 1601, and intended for a more general distribution than those printed on fine paper. At least one of the latter was a presentation copy.[5]

Nicholas Ling again brought books to Simmes, having brought

4. Arber III, 431.   5. Bodleian Arch Gd47, which has a
                                      dedication to the Library.

none for two years, although he had published several titles. This year Ling published three books, and Simmes printed them all, including an *Agnus Dei* (STC 25220), a thumb book which had the distinction of being the smallest book printed in England up to that date. Thomas Bushell, Ling's former apprentice, continued to give Simmes his work, and Felix Norton, another young Stationer who had become free two years before,[6] brought his only publishing venture of the year to Simmes.

Thomas Pavier continued to come to Simmes, giving him a series of news pamphlets on the siege of Ostend (STC 18893,4,4.1). There was a casual contact this year with a minor publisher, William Wood, for whom Simmes printed a religious work, *The Mirror of martyrs* (STC 25226). The last publisher in 1600 was Walter Burre, who commissioned *The Passions of the Mind* (STC 26039). Burre's right in this work is not clear. The title-page imprint is "printed by V.S. for W.B." However, as the book was entered by Simmes alone,[7] it would appear that the two men had reached some private arrangement about ownership.

In 1602 Simmes printed only slightly more than he had done the previous year. His linear total for the year was about 2500 meters, which is comparable to one large folio. Contracted printing fell off this year, but Simmes's personal publishing (three books, two of them theological) increased enough to off-set the loss.

Simmes again this year printed books for some of his standard publishers. Aspley handed over one short devotional book (STC 6336), as did Bushell (STC 20151). Ling brought two of his three books to Simmes, a satirical work by Greene (STC 12254.1) and Wright's *Display of Duty* (STC 26026). Clement Knight had not published any books since he had been to Simmes in 1596; this year he resumed publishing by bringing out a *New and short defence of tobacco* (STC 6469.1) which Simmes printed. Simon Waterson brought one book, Lodge's *Paradoxes against common opinions* (STC 16661).

Simmes continued to receive work from young, newly-established Stationers, this year printing two books for John Barnes, who had become a freeman the previous year.[8] There is a question with one of the books, Clapham's *History of England* (STC 5347), whether it was the property of Barnes or Simmes; although it was "Printed by Valentine Simmes, for John Barnes," it was entered in the Register in the normal way to Simmes alone.[9]

6. Arber II, 727.

7. Arber III, 185.

8. Arber II, 730.

9. Arber III, 201.

There was a casual contact with a John Bailey, for whom Simmes printed *A poetical rhapsody* (STC 6373). Morrison assigns four books in 1602 to John Bailey, but McKerrow mentions three men of the name publishing between 1600 and 1610. Little is known of any of them.

Production for 1603 shows a surprising increase, almost tripling the 1602 figures. Simmes's own publishing dwindled almost to nothing, but his contracted work reached over 6000 meters, the highest figure it ever reached. One does not have to search for the reason for this sudden increase: it was a single volume.

Edward Blount had contracted Simmes to print Montaigne's *Essays* (STC 18041) for him, a major publishing venture which, in linear measure, runs to more than 4700 meters, making up about three-quarters of Simmes's output for the year. Here again, however, we must be cautious. Blount entered the book in the Register in 1602[1] and Simmes could have begun work on it at any time after that date. The only point which suggests that the book was machined off within a reasonably short period of time is the paper used, which, although a job lot, was not used for any books prior to 1603, while some of the same watermarks do turn up in books printed a few months later.

This was not all Simmes printed for Blount; two other books, both thin folios, were printed as well. These were Daniel's *Panegyric Congratulatory* (STC 6258) which was followed by a re-issue from the same standing type, but adding the *Defence of ryme* (STC 6259).

The publishers who dealt with Simmes this year follow the usual pattern; a few who relied heavily on him for printing their books, and a number of younger men who brought a book or two at the beginning of their careers, but never returned. In 1603 there were more than the usual number of casual contacts. Three men who had done a small amount of business with Simmes before returned with a book each: Walter Burre, Thomas Millington, and Cuthbert Burby. Two minor Stationers, Edmund Mutton and James Shawe, came to Simmes this once only. It is unusual to find in this group of casual contacts the names of older, established publishers, yet this year two such men dealt with Simmes. Edward White Sr. brought one book, and John Harrison the Younger brought another. Actually, Simmes did not print all of Harrison's book, *A fruitful meditation* (STC 14377), but only the first sheet, the remainder having been farmed out to another printer.

Two other reliable customers came again in 1603. Clement Knight had Simmes print half his output for the year, all, as was usual, theological. Nicholas Ling contracted Simmes to print three of the four

1. Arber III, 152.

books he published this year. One of the books is of special interest, as it was the first quarto of *Hamlet* (STC 22275).

In 1604 Simmes's business continued to increase, and this year was, next to 1596, his busiest year, during which he set almost 7500 meters of type. His contracted work was down slightly from 1603, but his own publishing increased considerably, raising the total production figure.[2] Simmes himself published only one book this year, a Latin New Testament (STC 2811=3735). This was the largest publishing venture Simmes engaged in alone, running to almost 2000 meters of type, and accounting for over a quarter of his year's production.

Simmes this year printed a second book almost as long as the Testament. This was Acosta's *History of the East and West Indies* (STC 94), which he printed for Aspley and Blount. Both men came with other books also. Aspley commissioned a small theological book (STC 12058) and the Marston play, *The Malcontent* (STC 17479-81). Simmes printed three editions of the play this year, using some standing type for two of his quartos.[3]

Blount too handed over a play, one of William Alexander's *Monarchick Tragedies* (STC 343). Simmes printed *Croesus*, while the second play, *Darius,* was printed by George Elde. In addition to these books, Blount brought Ben Jonson's *Royal entertainment* (STC 14756); the three books made up about half of Blount's output for the year.

Simmes printed three more plays in 1604, each for a different publisher. For Matthew Law he reprinted *Henry IV Part I* (STC 22282); for Thomas Bushell he printed the first quarto of *Doctor Faustus* (STC 17429). For John Hodgets he printed part of the first quarto of Dekker's *The Honest Whore* (STC 6501); the first two sheets are Simmes's work, the remainder was farmed out to printers.[4]

The remainder of his business in 1604 was obtained from Walter Burre, for whom he reprinted an enlarged edition of *Passions of the mind* (STC 26040), and from Thomas Man, an older Stationer for whom Simmes printed a theological work, *The golden chain of salvation* (STC 20889).

Business again followed a downward trend in 1605. The contracted work fell off slightly, but Simmes's personal publishing dropped back to a more normal figure of a few hundred meters, so that his total setting was just under 5000 meters.

2. However, see the discussion on shared printing post p. 87ff.

3. But the discussion post p. 94ff.

4. For fuller discussion of this problem see Bowers: *The Dramatic Works of Thomas Dekker*, Vol.II, p.4.

Four publishers came to Simmes for the first time this year. Nathaniel Butter, who had begun to publish the previous year, came with three books, a third of his titles for the year. Matthew Lownes, who was by this time fairly well established, brought two of his five books to Simmes. The fact that Lownes had been apprenticed to Ling may have influenced his choice of printer. The third newcomer was William Leake who, in the middle of his career, had Simmes print Smith's *Four sermons* (STC 22766). Lastly, the young William Ferbrand gave Simmes the printing of a topical book, *The royal entertainment of the Earl of Nottingham* (STC 13857), one of the two books he published this year.

Nicholas Ling continued to hand over work to Simmes, this year giving him a long octavo, Drayton's *Poems* (STC 7216). Ling had more than his share of Drayton, for he was associated with slightly over half the poet's publications up to 1607, the year Ling ceased to publish.

There remain to mention only two casual printing jobs this year. One was a re-issue of *The Honest Whore* (STC 6502) for Hodgets, which consisted simply of cancelling the title-page and trying to sell off old stock. The other job was a short book reprinted for Matthew Law.

Simmes's business decline accelerated in 1606. His contracts shrank to a third the previous year's, and his personal publishing rose only slightly. The result was a drop from 5400 meters in 1605 to under 2400 meters in 1606. Only four publishers gave work to him in 1606. Nicholas Ling had Simmes print Erasmus's *Seven dialogues* (STC 10457) and reprint the tiny *Agnus Dei* (STC 25222). Nathaniel Butter, the young publisher who had first come to Simmes the previous year, was associated with Simmes in producing Hind's *Eliosto libidinoso* (STC 13509) which was printed by Simmes, to be sold by Butter. This arrangement leaves the identity of the publisher in doubt.

There were three casual printing jobs in 1606. One was the printing of a Barnaby Rich volume (STC 20983) for Geoffrey Chorlton, and the others were the printing of two small books for Thomas Thorpe. One of these was a play, the first quarto of Chapman's *The gentleman usher* (STC 4978), and the other was Jonson's *Hymenaei* (STC 14774). Thorpe's name had not appeared on any previous Simmes title-page, but he was involved in Marston's *Malcontent* which Simmes printed for Aspley, for in the Stationers' Register entry both Aspley and Thorpe are named as owners of the copy.

Simmes's 1607 production figures nearly equalled those of 1606. His personal publishing consisted of two fairly short books, and his contracted printing increased only slightly. Again, Nicholas Ling brought books to Simmes. Ling published five books this year, and Simmes printed three of them; these contracts made up over a quarter of his total production. One of the books was a play, a third quarto of *The taming of a shrew* (STC 23669).

It is interesting to note that this was Ling's last year of full-time publishing. Nothing is heard of him from November of the year when sixteen of his copies were transferred to John Smethwick,[4] until 1630 when he and Edward White published a single volume (STC 19192).

Edward Blount came to Simmes in 1607 after a lapse of three years, and brought two more of Alexander's *Monarchick Tragedies*. Simmes printed the two new plays, *The Alexandrine* and *Caesar*, and supplied a cancel title-page for unsold copies of the 1604 edition of *Croesus*. These three, with the fourth play, the 1604 *Darius*, were put forth as a new edition (STC 344). Yet another book was brought to Simmes, *The Fair Maid of the Exchange* (STC 13317).[5] It was brought by Henry Rockit, a small publisher, and printed without any reference to Simmes on the imprint. Matthew Lownes also came again to Simmes, having him print Lever's *Queen Elizabeth's tears* (STC 15540).

Three novices came to Simmes this year for the first time. John Budge began publishing this year, and brought one of his two books to Simmes. Two other new Stationers, Matthew Cooke and Samuel Macham, came together to Simmes to have him print the *Report of a bloody massacre in the city of Moscow* (STC 21461). Both of these men had begun publishing the previous year, when they jointly issued eight books. This year they published only one book jointly, as Cooke died.

Now we come to a blank in Simmes's career until 1610, when he had a single book, Thomas's *Seven Sinners* (STC 24005), reprinted for him by Thomas Purfoot; he printed nothing himself.[6] In 1611 Simmes's name is associated with three books. One book, *Poesy of floured prayers* (STC 5653) was printed for Simmes by an unnamed printer and sold by Edward White, an older Stationer. The other two were apparently printed *by* Simmes, but none of Simmes's old ornament stock was used.[7] One book was a small volume of verse (STC

4. Arber III, 365. A few months later, in Feb. 1611, Ling's *Agnus Dei* was entered to Smithwick with Simmes' consent: Arber III, 452.

5. Again I am indebted to Mr Wyllie for bringing this book to my attention.

6. There is in STC an entry of a book printed by Simmes in 1610. This entry, STC 3059, proved to be a ghost entry, and the book referred to was actually printed in 1605, as STC 3058.

7. The third quarto of *Hamlet* (STC 22277) has been attributed to Simmes, but see discussion post p. 90.

15227) published for yet another new Stationer, Richard Bonian. The other book was an edition of *The troublesome raigne of King John* (STC 14646) which Simmes printed for John Helme, who, incidentally, had been apprenticed to Ling.

Finally, in 1612, Simmes engaged in his last publishing venture. This was the *History of . . . Mervine* (STC 17844) which was printed jointly by Simmes and Ralph Blower. Simmes's relationship with Blower is not known; perhaps he came into partial partnership with him, or perhaps worked with him as a journeyman. The book itself, however, shows none of the careful workmanship associated with a Simmes publication.

It is possible to come to a few general conclusions about Simmes's business history. It was an unsteady business, judged in terms of typesetting. It had two periods of great activity; the single year 1596 and the three year period from 1603 to 1605. After these peaks were several slack years, when production was cut to a fraction of the peak years'. The more surprising peak is, of course, that of 1596, when Simmes had been printing and publishing for only two years. Why a new business should spurt ahead immediately and then fall back as suddenly is a matter for conjecture.

It was not a large business; many of Simmes's contemporaries, such as Thomas Creede or Felix Kingston, printed three or more times the amount Simmes's press produced. However, many of the books which he did print are now of primary literary importance. His plays, including eight Shakespeare quartos, *Faustus*, and *Shoemakers' Holiday*, are important to us, and the publication of Montaigne's *Essays* was a literary landmark.

Two points strike us concerning the publishers who came to Simmes. First, there were few publishers who gave him very much business, and second, they were, in the main, young and inexperienced men in their first years of business. Of the 48 individual publishers with whom Simmes dealt, only eight of them — Adams, Aspley, Blount, Busby, Bushell, Butter, Ling, and Wise — had Simmes print more than five books for them. Simmes printed single volumes for no fewer than 26 of his publishers.

The youth of Simmes's publishers is conspicuous throughout his career. Of the 48 publishers who came to him, 25 of them, just over half, had been in business for three years or less. The remainder of his publishers were relatively young also; only five of his publishers had been in business for twenty years or more when they first came to Simmes, and another five had been established for between ten and twenty. Even these men need not have been men much older than Simmes. For example, Nicholas Ling, who was a near contemporary, had been publishing for fourteen years when Simmes began printing in 1594.

The importance of Nicholas Ling in Simmes's business has been obvious. Ling commissioned Simmes to print about a third of his books for him, and several other publishers who came to Simmes had been Ling's apprentices. It is an interesting coincidence that both men stopped their activities with equal suddenness, at the same time, although there is as yet no evidence connecting the two events.

Chapter III*

The Compositors of *Henry IV, Part 2, Much Ado About Nothing, The Shoemakers' Holiday,* and *The First Part of the Contention*

We have noticed that Simmes printed several plays, and famous titles have appeared as we have followed his career. Dramatic texts provide an excellent vehicle for the study of compositors, as there is a minimum of justification and a maximum of variety in setting techniques: stage directions, speech-prefixes, names, etc. In 1600 alone Simmes printed four important dramatic quartos. These form a convenient unit for study, as they were all printed within a short period of time and, with *The Contention*, we have the added attraction of having the copy available for comparison. The following is a study of their compositors.

The first quarto of *2 Henry IV* was set by a single compositor. This can be demonstrated from several typographical and spelling peculiarities, but most forcefully by a single idiosyncrasy not generally observed in books of the period. When the compositor of an Elizabethan dramatic text set speech-prefixes, whether abbreviated or unabbreviated, it was usual for him to put a stop after the prefix, thus setting it off from the following text. An examination of the dramatic texts printed from manuscript in the three years 1599, 1600, and 1601 illustrates the general acceptance of this convention. There were 28 plays[1] printed for the first time in these years, 22 of them by printers other than Simmes. Prefixes without stops after them did occasionally appear: there were two in *Two Angry Women of Abingdon*, and two more in *Jack Drum's Entertainment*. In two of the plays where numbers were used as prefixes, there were occasional unstopped tags.[2] No other unstopped prefixes appeared in the 22 texts.

In the first quarto of *2 Henry IV* this convention was completely reversed; in almost every case where a full name is used as a speech-prefix there is no mark of punctuation after it. Unabbreviated prefixes appear in 69 of the 80 pages of the text; there are 335 such prefixes and in all but five of these occurrences there is no stop after the prefix. The speech-prefixes occur in the text as follows:

	A2	v	3	v	4	v	B1	v	2	v	3	v	4	v	C1	v
Abbreviated:	—	4	3	3	4		6		10	12	18	2		8	10	6
full, unstopped:	—	3	4	4	2	1	2	3	8	3		5	8	1		8
full, stopped:		1														

*Reprinted with permission from *Studies in Bibliography* XIII (1960).

1. As found in W. W. Greg, *A Bibliography of the English Printed Drama to the Restoration*, Nos. 155-182.

2. *Everyman Out of his Humor* and *Old Fortunatus*.

2	v	3	v	4	v	D1	v	2	v	3	v	4	v	E1	v	2	v	3	v	4	v
9	7	13	5		2	3	3	3	5	10	8	13	13	13	6	8	8	8	16	13	13
7		5	15	9	14	11	19	4	3	4	2	2	1	3	9	10	7	5	1	1	1
														1		1					

F1	v	2	v	3	v	4	v	G1	v	2	v	3	v	4	v	H1	v	2	v	3	v
22	18	16	12	7	2	2	4	5	4	3	3	7	4	7	8	2	8	3	2	9	11
2	5	1	2		3	6	3	3	1	2	3	8	7		7	1	4	3	2		7
								1													

4	v	I1	v	2	v	3	v	4	v	K1	v	2	v	3	v	4	v	L1	v
6	1			5	7	10	11	5		1	8	14	9	7	14	7	8	—	
5	3	1		1	7	7		5	3	1		8	9	10	6	3	2	8	—
													1						

There are other typographical features in this text which, in their uniformity, both attest to setting by a single compositor and exhibit some of his typographical characteristics. We note first that the compositor does not distinguish names, titles, or territories by setting them in a contrasting type-fount. Thus the body of the text is in roman with no italic type introduced into it (except for four Latin words), and on the other hand the speech-prefixes and stage directions are set wholly in italic.

In 2 *Henry IV* there is a sparing use of emphasis capitals and of parentheses: both are found where a reader would expect to find them in a modern text. The result is that the type-pages have an even and regular appearance; the body of the text is set in a single fount unbroken by the interspersal of italic type or superfluous capital letters. It is always a neat and well planned page.

The stage-directions are treated in a regular way. Apart from exits, there are 58 stage-directions in the text. Forty-two are centred on the page, and in all but two of the centred directions the initial letter is a capital. Where the directions are flush right, half have capitals and half have lower-case initial letters. All directions end with periods.

There are 17 exits in this text, all in correct Latin. They consist of the words *exit* or *exeunt* (occasionally abbreviated) and sometimes the names of the characters concerned. No exits are centred; most (13) are placed at the end of a line, but four are set slightly in from the right-hand margin. Only three exits do not end with stops. Whereas the centred stage-directions almost invariably begin with capitals, the practice with exits is to use a lower-case 'e.' Only one exit begins with a capital.

The catchwords are notable for brevity. Only one word is used as a catchword, and in the one instance where the rather long word, "inuincible" is to be the catchword, only the first two syllables, "inuin-" are given. As often happens in a dramatic text, speech-prefixes form many catchwords; in no case is the first word of the speech also given in the catchword.

The signatures are regular throughout the book. They consist of a roman capital, arabic numeral, no stop, and a narrow quad between letter and number. The signature is always set with the catchword on a separate line, but there is no set positioning of the signature in relation to margins or the beginning of the catchword.

A spelling analysis of this text yields results which support the view that it was set by a single compositor. Where two or more compositors are at work in a text, spellings peculiar to each man tend in analysis to separate out and occur mainly on the pages set by that workman. In *2 Henry IV* the spelling variants occur at random throughout the text and fail to conform to any bibliographical units. An examination of the verse passages alone also produces a random scattering of variants; ten words occur in this text in which the spelling variations make little or no difference to their length, but these again provide no recognizable pattern.

Another method of attempting to distinguish compositors by spelling habits is to examine classes of variants which are subject to habitual treatment. This is especially valuable in a prose text, where large numbers of variants will form a definite pattern. Three classes of variants were examined: the use of a final letter '*e*', -*ie*/-*y* variants, and -*ll*/*l* variants.

An examination and tabulation of all variants in these classes shows that throughout this text there is a marked preference for one form of the variant over the other. In the cases where the final '*e*' could be retained or dropped, the preference was to drop it; this was observed in 296 out of 441 cases, a 65% preference for the shorter form. With -*ie*/-*y* the preference again is for the shorter form. Final '-*y*' was used 115 times and final '-*ie*' 52: a 69% preference for the '-*y*' variant. With -*ll*/*l* on the other hand, the longer form is preferred with even higher consistency. Single '-*l*' is used 115 times and the double form 340. The percentage preference is 74%.

There is a slight pattern exhibited by some of the variant classes, but none is very pronounced. With the final '*e*' variant there is a slight tendency for the longer form to be more prevalent in prose than in verse passages. A faint pattern emerges with the -*ll*/*l* variant. Occasionally in verse passages there is a tendency for the '-*ll*' form to drop slightly. The -*ie*/-*y* variants show no pattern.

The spelling analysis of this text does not show a pattern of two or more compositors, but rather shows that in the three classes of variant a preferential pattern pervades the entire text, supporting the hypothesis that one man set the entire play.

On similar evidence the first quarto of *Much Ado about Nothing* can be assigned to one compositor. As the points observed coincide exactly with those observed in *2 Henry IV*, it is almost certain that the same compositor set both plays.

Again unabbreviated speech-headings give the strongest evidence. Unabbreviated headings appear on all but four pages of text; there are 489 of them, and only two have stops after them. The speech-prefixes occur as follows:

	A2	v	3	v	4	v	B1	v	2	v	3	v	4	v	C1	v
Abbreviated:	9	13	13	13	10	9	7	2	7	6	3		4	20	6	3
Full, unstopped:		2	5	2	6	9	7	6	6	6	12	10	14	4	9	11
Full, stopped:																

	2	v	3	v	4	v	D1	v	2	v	3	v	4	v	E1	v	2	v	3	v	4	v
	1		9	3	6	4	6	9	10		6	1		1	10	11	11	3	1	11	14	
	6	15	8	10	6	3	6	5	7	17	9	1	7	6	10	6	9	8	13	13	6	1
					1																	

	F1	v	2	v	3	v	4	v	G1	v	2	v	3	v	4	v	H1	v	2	v	3	v
	8	11	13	11	6	2	5	1	5	1	1	13	23	9	8		1		16	7	4	
	10	5	3	7	13	13	12	12	3	5	2	1		9	13	12	4	14	13	6	4	11
																						1

	4	v	I1	v	2	v	3	v	4	v
	8	2	14	11	14	2	13	13	15	5
	6	4	3		1	8	5	4	2	

This alone is conclusive evidence that the single compositor of *2 Henry IV* set this play as well; all other evidence is corroborative.

Again there is no unnecessary mixing of roman and italic type in the text of *Much Ado*. Only when a Latin tag is used on F2 is italic type introduced into the roman text. Similarly there is no roman type used in the stage-directions. The same even appearance of the type-page due to sparing use of emphasis capitals and parentheses is seen here as in *2 Henry IV*.

The regular treatment of the stage-directions (again excluding exits) is more pronounced in *Much Ado* than in *2 Henry IV*. There are 43 stage-directions, 38 of which are centred and begin with capital letters. Of the five directions which are set flush right, four begin with capitals and one with lower case.

There are 24 regular exits in the quarto and their treatment is the same as in 2 *Henry IV*. Twenty-two of these begin with a lower case 'e'. Eight exits are at the end of a line, while 16 are slightly indented. Full stops are usual, appearing after all but five. In four additional cases the exit is treated as a regular stage-direction, centred and capitalized. This possibly reflects some influence from the copy.

Catchwords again are brief. Only one word is used as a catchword; the first word of a speech is never added when a speech-prefix forms the catchword. Again, as in 2 *Henry IV*, there are cases where long catchwords have been shortened: "mortifying" is cut to "mor-" and "Conuerting" to "Con-".

A complete spelling analysis again corroborates the evidence pointing to single-compositor setting. Variants throughout the text, variants in verse passages, and variants involving little or no change in the length of the word all appeared at random.

An examination of the three classes of variants — final 'e', -ie/-y, and -ll/l — shows again a strong preference for one form of the variant over the other. In 73% of the variant cases the final 'e' was dropped, in 75% the longer '-ll' was preferred to '-l' and in 77% of the variant forms '-y' endings were preferred to '-ie'.

The second quarto of *The First Part of the Contention* was printed by Simmes in 1600 from a copy of Q1, which had been printed by Creede in 1594. Since most of Q2 exhibits the same typographical features as 2 *Henry IV* and *Much Ado*, we may infer that most of it was set by the same compositor, but that formes A outer, A inner, and B outer were set by an alternate workman.

Again the speech-prefixes provide the strongest argument for identifying the compositor. On B inner and from sig. C to the end of the text there are 338 unabbreviated speech-prefixes, of which 276 are unstopped and 62 stopped. On three pages of the text there is no evidence as no unabbreviated prefixes appear. The distribution of prefixes is as follows:

	A2	v	3	v	4	v	B1	v	2	v	3	v	4	v	C1	v
Abbreviated:	—	2	2	6	3	2	4	1	5	1	6	9	2	2	6	10
Full, unstopped:	—						1		3	6	1	5	4	1	4	5
Full, stopped:	—		8	2	2	2	4	2	3	3	7	1	2	4	4	1

2	v	3	v	4	v	D1	v	2	v	3	v	4	v	E1	v	2	v	3	v	4	v
15	7	8	4	1	3	2	6	8	3	4	1	5	5	4	5	4	4	8	6	3	1
7	25	6	5	2	2	5	8	3	3	6	5	3	3	8	8	2	6	3	2	2	3
1						2				1				1		2		1	2	1	1

F1	v	2	v	3	v	4	v	G1	v	2	v	3	v	4	v	H1	v	2	v	3	v	4
3	5	11	12	1				3	4	1	1	3	5			3	4	1	7	7	4	4
3	5	5	1	9	16	8	7	7	7	7	10	4	2	6	5	6	8	9		3	3	1
1		7	4	5	2	2		2	5	1	5	2	1									

It should be pointed out that in this text the compositors were working from printed copy, and were sometimes influenced by it. The speech-prefixes in Q1 were all stopped, except for three tags on C3.

Signature A and the outer forme of sig. B are distinguished by stopped prefixes. In sig. A there are 15 unabbreviated prefixes, 14 of them stopped. In outer B, 18 of the 20 unabbreviated prefixes have periods; by contrast inner B has 26 unabbreviated prefixes and the pattern is reversed, only 8 being stopped and the remaining 18 unstopped.

Other evidence indicates a change of compositors between B inner and outer. In 2 *Henry IV* and *Much Ado* the exits are usually begun with a lower-case 'e'. In sig. A and outer B of *The Contention* there are eleven exits, seven of which begin with a capital 'E'. In inner B and from sig. C to the end of the text there are 54 exits, and all but one begin with a lower-case 'e'. The single exception can be dismissed as it is the beginning of a lengthy stage-direction.

Both 2 *Henry IV* and *Much Ado* are characterized by the use of a single fount of type in the body of the text, without any use of a contrasting fount for names or titles. This practice is followed consistently in inner B and succeeding sheets, and is a deliberate departure from the copy-text where names are regularly set off in a contrasting type-face. In sheet A and outer B italic type is introduced into the roman in setting 25 names.

Throughout this text the treatment of the stage directions and catchwords follows the patterns seen in 2 *Henry IV* and *Much Ado*. Most stage-directions are centred and begin with capitals; both compositors occasionally follow their copy and set stage directions in roman. Catchwords are brief, and again there are cases where a single word has been cut: "Prefageth" to "Prefa-", "Warwicke" to "War-", and "Immortall" to "Immor-".

Enough evidence has now been adduced to support the inference that two compositors were at work in Simmes's shop. The workman in 1600 who set all of 2 *Henry IV, Much Ado*, and most of *The Contention* and whom we have distinguished through his unusual habit of leaving unabbreviated speech-prefixes unstopped, may be referred to as Compositor A. The workman who set sig. A and outer B of *The Contention* may be referred to as Compositor B. Although only three formes of his work, involving ten pages of text, have been examined, his work can be distinguished from that of Compositor A by his tendency to capitalize his exits.

Q2 of *The Contention* offers an opportunity of examining the work of the Simmes compositors more closely, as it was set from a copy of the first quarto of 1594, with which it can be collated. A collation reveals several tendencies shared by the two compositors. Both, for example, failed to reproduce emphasis capitals in their copy. This is a practice expected of them after the even, unbroken type-pages of *2 Henry IV* and *Much Ado*. In Q1 of *The Contention* there are many words, such as Lord, Lady, Prince, and Crown, which are regularly capitalized. Just as regularly both compositors of Q2 replaced these emphasis capitals with lower-case, changing 278 in the course of the play. There are 31 cases in which capitals have been added, but these were mostly where punctuation changes demanded it.

Throughout the text punctuation marks were changed seemingly at the compositors' discretion. The following table records all changes in punctuation, indicating whether the changes were toward heavier or lighter punctuation, or in the case of changes in full stops, retained the same value. The first number indicates changes in A's stint; a second number denotes B's.

HEAVIER		*LIGHTER*	
no stop to comma	109-20	full stop to colon	52
no stop to colon	1	full stop to comma	42-4
no stop to full stop	4	full stop to no stop	4
comma to colon	13-2	colon to comma	5-2
comma to full stop	17-1	comma to no stop	39-8
colon to full stop	1		—
	—		156
	178		

FULL-STOP VARIANTS

period to question mark	16-8
period to exclamation mark	6-1
question mark to period	1
	—
	32

There is a tendency here toward heavier punctuation, but it is cancelled out in large measure by the removal of stops or their reduction. The most obvious increase is that while 51 stops have been removed entirely, 144 have been introduced into the text, a net increase of 93. The colon and comma are the preferred stops, with a net increase of 60 colons and 112 commas. Q1 had been lax in its use of question marks, but Q2 supplied them regularly.

These observations help one give a qualified yes to Alice Walker's query, "Did Simmes normally pepper his texts with the heavy metrical pointing exemplified in the verse of 2 *Henry IV* and *Much Ado*?"[3] It is also important to an editor of a Simmes quarto to know that these compositors did take such a free hand with punctuation, especially with the less common colon.

Changes involving final 'e', -ie/-y, and -ll/l variations were made by both compositors. In 152 cases the compositors dropped the final 'e' of their copy, and 57 times they added it. The -ie/-y changes were more marked, for 71 times the -ie ending of the copy was changed to -y: only once was the opposite change made. Both practices are to be expected from the compositor who set 2 *Henry IV* and *Much Ado*. But the tendency in treating -ll/-l variants runs counter to the practice of the other texts. The shorter form is preferred to the longer, with 78 -ll forms being shortened and only 26 -l forms being lengthened to -ll. All three tendencies were noted proportionally in the work set by each compositor, thus reducing the value of ending-preferences in determining compositors. Although admittedly slim evidence, it is observed that Compositor B was responsible for slightly more than his share of added final 'e' forms, and was responsible for the single -ie to -y change.

Several spelling changes were made by the compositors, most of them modernizations. The most important are tabulated below. The number of times the change was made appears beside each variant. Where only one number is given, it denotes the number of occurrences in Compositor A's stint; where two numbers, the first represents A and the second B:

eye (s) to eie (s)	8-3	cleare to cleere	4-1
bene to bin	7	unkle to unckle	5
bene to beene	8-3	honour to honor	7
proud (e) to prowd	12-7	soldiers to souldiers	5
blood to bloud	14	troopes to troup (e) s	4

Distinguishing the two compositors is rendered more difficult because they had similar spelling habits, and both treated emphasis capitals, full stage-directions, and catchwords in the same ways. These similarities throw greater importance upon the treatment of speech-prefixes and exits as means of distinguishing them, and the evidence these

3. Alice Walker, *Textual Problems in the First Folio* (1953), p. 163.

afford must be backed up by any other idiosyncracies which occur in a particular text.

A fourth dramatic text set in Simmes's workshop in 1600 was the first quarto of *The Shoemakers' Holiday*. It was set by two compositors. One of the compositors was A; there is only slight evidence that the other compositor was B.

On the basis of the treatment of speech-prefixes, the following passages can be assigned to Compositor A: four speeches on B4, all of C1 and C1v, the bottom of G1v and the remainder of the inner forme of sheet G, and from sig. H to the end of the play. The remainder of the play was set by another compositor, with the possible exception of sheet A which cannot be assigned for lack of evidence.

Professor Bowers in his compositorial analysis of this play has noticed the spelling and speech-prefix evidence and used it in helping to assign some of the pages to an alternate compositor. He writes:

. . . the compositor of B1-3v carefully placed full stops after each speech-heading, but suddenly in the middle of B4 four such headings in a row are not punctuated. The stops return on B4v but they are totally absent in all speech-prefixes on C1 and C1v; thereafter, the tags are consistently punctuated until towards the foot of G1v again no stops are found, and this lack of punctuation continues on G2, skips to G3v, and is found sporadically on G4. Full stops are consistent on G4v, but sporadic from H1 to the end of the play. On B4, in the section wanting stops, for the first time a character's name is set in roman instead of black letter, and on C1 and C1v all names are in roman but thereafter in black letter until roman appears again on G2, H3v, and I4 inconsistently, but consistently on K3. The fact that on G2 occurs the spelling *Rafe* (5 times), and *Sibil* (8 times), but on G2v *Raph* (5 times) and *Sibil* (5 times; *Sibil* once) seems to confirm a change of compositors at this point, in spite of the fact that the variant spellings of these names are of little assistance elsewhere.[4]

The four speeches in the middle of B4 are characterized by the absence of stops after the prefixes, and by some spelling changes which are in addition to those noted by Bowers. The usual 'Lord' is twice dropped to 'lord', the spelling 'Mayor' is introduced in place of the usual 'Maior', and 'Lacie' becomes 'Lacy.'

Bowers also correctly identifies C1 and C1v as the work of this compositor. On these pages there are ten speech-prefixes — all unabbreviated and unstopped. There is a continuation of the practice of setting names in roman, with 7 examples on C1 and 4 on C1v. 'Lacie' becomes 'Lacy' the four times it appears, 'Lord' is reduced to 'lord'

4. *The Dramatic Works of Thomas Dekker*, I (1953) 12-13.

once, and once *'Maior'* becomes *'Mayor.'* The usage is not consistent as both *'Lord'* and *'Maior'* appear as well.

Compositor A began again at the foot of G1v. Bowers follows him to the end of G2, but the evidence of the unstopped prefixes takes up again on G3v and G4, thus completing the inner forme.

The last five speeches on G1v have unabbreviated unstopped speech-prefixes, but no further evidence. On G2, in addition to all of the 17 unabbreviated prefixes being unstopped, there is one name set in roman and the spelling *'Mayor'* is used both times the word appears. Bowers points out the importance here of the *Raph/Rafe* spellings which seem to confirm a compositor change at G2/G2v. By the same evidence Compositor A took up again on G3v, for on G3 the spelling *'Raph'* appears six times and on G3v *'Rafe'* appears five, thus providing the pattern:

	G2	G2v	G3	G3v
Raph		5	6	
Rafe	5			5

The three sheets, H, I, and K can be assigned to Compositor A on the evidence of speech-prefix treatment. There are 189 unabbreviated speech-prefixes on these pages, and 177 are unstopped, with only 12 stopped prefixes appearing sporadically. The pattern of speech-prefixes for the entire text is as follows:

	B1	v	2	v	3	v	4	v	C1	v	2	v	3	v	4	v
Abbreviated:	1		2													3
Full, unstopped:			1				4		5	6						
Full, stopped:	3	2	5	5	11	10	8	6			3	9	11	15	9	7

D1	v	2	v	3	v	4	v	E1	v	2	v	3	v	4	v	F1	v	2	v	3	v
12	6	1		1	4	5	2	8	2	1	1	4	1			1	2			1	8
					1					1			1		1				1		
14	13	10	10	12	9	7	3	6	11	4	10	12	10	11	7	9	9	4	13	7	9

4	v	G1	v	2	v	3	v	4	v	H1	v	2	v	3	v	4	v	I1	v	2	v
7	5	8	1		3	4	1	2	5	3	7	7	6	8				4	4	9	10
		5	17		1	1	9	3		2	7	6	3	5	6	6	6	14	6	6	8
7	5	8	11		8	5				3	6	3	1	1	2			1		1	1

3	v	4	v	K1	v	2	v	3	v	4	v
5	2			5	6	2	1				
7	7	11	10	7	7	10	14	6	9	12	1
1						1					

The absence of abbreviated speech-prefixes in large sections of the play is due, of course, to the names of Eyre and his apprentices, which are rarely abbreviated.

Spelling evidence in determining the compositors of this play is weak, as might be expected from the results in *The Contention*. A few preferences do stand out, however. Compositor A always uses the spelling '*Rafe*' and it appears 41 times in his stint. The other compositor is not consistent in his usage, setting '*Rafe*' 21 times and '*Raph*' 20. Compositor A occasionally lapses into setting names in roman within a black letter text, doing so 26 times; the other compositor did this only once on B4v. Compositor A uses the spelling '*Mayor*' nine times, although he preferred '*Maior*': the other compositor spelled '*Maior*' consistently.

There are marked preferences between the two compositors in their usage of *-ie/y* and *-ll/l*. Compositor A preferred the *-y* form, employing it in 104 of 172 cases, a 60% usage. The other compositor preferred the *-ie* form, using it 126 times out of 214, a 41% usage of the *-y* form, markedly different from that of A. The two men were not as far apart in their use of *-ll/l*; both preferred the longer form, Compositor A using it 64% of the time, the other compositor 52%.

In the short passage of *The Contention* which had been set by Compositor B we noticed only one characteristic which might help in identifying him elsewhere. He capitalized seven of the eleven exits in his stint of *The Contention*. In *Shoemaker* there are 44 exits. The twelve which fall in Compositor A's stint are, with the exception of the final exit, begun with the customary lower-case '*e.*' Of the 32 exits in the remainder of the text 13 are capitalized. This practice suggests slim evidence upon which it might be assigned to Compositor B.

These compositors set other plays too, of course. My purpose at this point is simply to identify them, and for this reason I have chosen a single year in which these men were very active, and within which time one could assume that their habits would remain relatively constant. I fully anticipate that others will take their lead from this study and apply these identifications to other Simmes dramatic quartos.[3]

3. For one such extension, see Charlton Hinman: "Shakespeare's Text — Then, Now and Tomorrow," *Shakespeare Survey* 18 (1965), p.27.

Chapter IV

Type-Founts, Ornaments, and Paper.

1.   TYPE-FOUNTS

Simmes used thirteen separate founts of type for printing the texts of his books, and also possessed some larger founts of letters used on title-pages and head-titles. The most common fount was one measuring 82mm.[1] and Simmes had this size in roman, italic, and black letter. The roman (referred to as R.1) was used from 1595, and during the first few years was used mainly for prefatory matter, and not as the principal fount. However, by 1597 it had established itself as Simmes's most commonly used fount, and was used in almost half his books, usually as the principal fount.

The black letter (B.L.1) of the same size was another popular fount. Strangely enough, this was never used to print prefatory matter, but always as the principal fount in a book. It was used most commonly in the earlier years, becoming less popular after 1601. Simmes printed about a fifth of his books with this fount.

Simmes also had an italic type (It.1) of the same size. This was used primarily for prefatory matter, and only once (STC 702.1:*1605*) was it used as the principal fount.

Simmes had slightly larger founts of roman and italic which he used frequently. The roman (R.2) measured 93mm. and was popular from the beginning of Simmes's career. It was frequently used as the principal fount of a book, although it was not used at all from 1600 to 1603. The italic equivalent (It.2) measured 94mm. and was used as a secondary fount, except for one book (STC 15355; *1603*) where it was used as the principal fount. Simmes did not have a black letter fount of this size.

There were three founts of slightly smaller size in regular use in Simmes's shop. The roman (R.4) measured 68mm. and was used as a secondary fount until 1597 when it was used as the principal fount in one book (STC 24097). It was not used again until 1600, but thereafter it was used regularly both as secondary and primary fount. The italic fount (It.4) measured 67mm., was used in only four books, and the black letter (B.L.3) of the same size was used only in 1596 and 1597.

---

1. All measurements are of 20 lines of type.

Simmes had two founts even smaller than these which he used occasionally. One was a roman (R.5) measuring 53mm., and the other was a black letter (B.L.2) measuring 54mm.

There were three larger founts which were used occasionally. One was a roman (R.3) measuring 111mm. used usually as a secondary fount, but occasionally used as the principal fount in folios. There was another larger roman (R.6) which measured 143mm. and used occasionally for printing prefatory matter. There was a matching italic (It.3) which was used for the same purpose.

Let us look more closely at his most frequently used types, his 82s. ROMAN 1: Simmes' early roman 82 (designated R.1a) can be distinguished by several characteristics, the most obvious being that the dot over the 'i' is slightly to the left of centre. There are other printers of the period who had an 82 with the 'dot left', but there are further idiosyncrasies which distinguish one fount from another. Simmes's supply of the letter 'p' for instance is a mixed one, with some of the letters inking heavily, some lightly, but most pieces marked by a heavy descender. Look, for example, at the first page of *Richard III*, lines 24 and 25, where the variable quality of this letter is evident. (The most easily accessible facsimile reprint of this play is in the Shakespeare Quarto Facsimile series.) There is one book printed probably in 1594 (STC 709) which does not have the heavy 'p' mixed in with the others. This suggests that Simmes supplemented his supply at that time, as books printed thereafter show the heavier forms. The letter 'g' in this fount is of fairly common, but distinct, variety, with the lower loop larger than the other, and with the end of the loop just barely touching to complete the circle. The letter 'k' is a wide one which fits well with the rest of the fount, but is easily distinguished from the narrow 'k' which is found in several other printers' 'dot left' founts. Creede, for example, had a mixed lot of 'k's as can be readily seen in the facsimile of *Henry V* at A2v. A glance again at *Richard III*, at G4v-H1, will show some of these differences, as the second printer used a narrow 'k', a 'g' with much less distinction in the size of the loops, and an 'i' with the dot in the centre.

It is not yet known where Simmes obtained his types, but this fount bears marks of resemblance with William How's 82. Over the years changes were made in the fount. A 'j' was added, and some 'centre dot' 'i's appeared by 1604. However, by 1606 Simmes had another fount of 82 characterized by centre dots on all the 'i's, rather a deep and narrow 'w', a slight flattening on the bottom of the lower loop of the 'g', and a pronounced serif on the descender of the 'q'. The new fount, designated as R.1b, which gives a much cleaner appearance than the old, can be seen in conjunction with R.1a in John Hind's *Eliosto Libidinoso* (STC 13509), printed in 1606. One section of the book, from D3 to E4v, was printed with R.1a, while the remainder was printed with R.1b. The division suggests that one compositor used one fount and, for this occasion at least, a second compositor used the other.

For the next year, until his materials were dispersed, Simmes used the newer fount in four books, apparently putting aside the older type. Some of the R.1a appears to have been handed on to Ballard, for he used an 82 with some 'dot left' to print STC 7493 in 1608.

ITALIC 1: Simmes began in 1595 with an italic 82 (designated It. 1a) which was characterized by two forms of 'w', a 'v' with the first minim ascending above the body of the letter, a 'y' with a markedly rounded tail, and two slightly differing forms of 'p'. This was used exclusively until 1596, when there appeared another italic 82 (It.1b) which did not have any of the variations in the 'w' or 'p', had a loop in the first minim of the 'v', and a less rounded tail on the 'y'. This fount is found in one book printed in 1596, but thereafter is used almost exclusively. The other fount is found occasionally in later years, being used, for example, for stage directions and prefixes in *Richard III*.

BLACK LETTER 1: At the beginning of his career Simmes used two founts of black letter measuring 82 mm. One of these was a crisp, new-looking fount, characterized by sharp detail and small forks at the tops of most ascenders. There appear to have been no tied letters in this fount, and most of the 'T's were rounded, although there were a few square 'T's mixed in with it. This fount, designated B.L.1a, was used in 1594 and '95, and extensively in 1596. However, only one book bearing a 1597 imprint date (STC 17323) was printed with it, and after this it was not employed again. It did seem to wear slightly through these brief years, but it is difficult to suggest why it was discarded.

The other black letter 82, designated as B.L.1b, was much less fresh in appearance. The ascenders were blunt at the ends, there were tied 'ee' and 'oo' available, and the 'T's were square (except in STC 4042 in 1595 where they appear to have been mixed with the other fount's round ones). This fount was first used in 1594, and after the disappearance of B.L.1a became Simmes' only 82 in this face, and was used throughout his career, although it did drop in popularity as roman became more standard over the years.

The following lists give the date and STC number of every book in which the particular fount appears. If the number is enclosed in square brackets, the type was used for prefatory matter only.

ROMAN 1. 20ll.=82mm.   1595: [3314], [4102], [15638];   1596: 1828,
[1829], 19180, [20797], [22971], [23361], [23362];   1597: 22307,
22314, [24097];   1598: 1047, 17760, [21311], 22308;   1599: 4987,
18370, [25089], 25224;   1600: 3675, 3679, [6523], [6798], 11578,
18795, 22288, 22304;   1601: [19343], 22736, 25765, 26039;   1602:
2771, 5347, [6336], 17621, 24004, [26026];   1603: 7084, 7085,
7539, 13848, 18041, 20170, 21467;   1604: 6501, 17479, 17480,
17481, 22282;   1605: [702.1], 6457, 6502, 7216, 15448, 21717,
22766;   1606: 4978, 13509, 14774;   1607: [710], 6785, 11842,
15535, [15540];   1611: 14646(?).

ROMAN 2. 20ll.=93mm.   1595: 3314, [4101], 22954, 22972, 23361;
1596: [13252];   1597: [17323], 17906;   1598: 3216;   1599: 17994,
26019;   1603: 3068, 5121, 6259, [14377];   1604: 94, 343, 12058,
14756, [17480], 20889, 26040;   1605: 3058, 6071;   1606: 5348,
20983;   1607: 344, [6785], [15535], 15540, 23669.

ROMAN 3. 20ll.=111mm.   1594: [22860];   1598: [3216];   1599:
[26019];   1601: 6236, 6237;   1602: [2771], [17621], [26026];
1603: [5121], 6258, [6259];   1605: 1457, [3058], 13857].

ROMAN 4. 20ll.=68mm.   1596: [720], [1829], [14802], [15281],
[19180];   1597: 24097;   1600: 24152;   1601: 25226, [26039];
1602: 20151;   1603: [5121], 13592, [13848], [25221];   1604:
[2811], [14756], [20889];   1605: [7216];   1606: [14774], [25222];
1607: [6785].

ROMAN 5. 20ll.=53mm.   1595: 3012;   1596: [23362].

ROMAN 6. 20ll.=143mm.   1596: [1053], [17126.1];   1597: [17906];
1603: [6259].

ITALIC 1. 20ll.=82mm.   1595: [4042], [4102], [19180], [22954];
1596: [720], [1829], [13252], [22972];   1598: [12099], [21311];
1599: [25224], [26019];   1600: [18795];   1601: [25226];   1602:
[2771], [24004];   1604: [2811], [17481], [20889], [26040];   1605:
702.1, [7216], [22766];   1606: [13509], [14774], [20983];   1607:
[11842], [15540].

ITALIC 2. 20ll.=94mm.   1595: [4101], [19180], [23361];   1596:
[20797], [22972];   1600: [3675];   1601: [6236], [6237];   1602:
[5347];   1603: [3068], [7084], [7085], 15355;   1604: [343],
[14756], [20889];   1605: [1457];   1606: [20983];   1607: [344],
[11842], [15535].

ITALIC 3. 20ll.=143mm.   1594: [709];   1595: [3314], [22954];   1600:
[3679], [11578];   1602: [17621];   1603: [13848];   1607: [710],
[15540].

ITALIC 4. 20ll.=67mm.   1597: [24097];   1600: [24152];   1601:
[25226];   1603: [13592].

BLACK LETTER 1. 20ll.=82mm.   **1594**: 709, 22860;   **1595**: 4042,
4101, 4102, 15638, 23361;   **1596**: 720, 1053, 1829, 13252, 14802,
15281, 17126.1, 20797, 23362;   **1597**: 15379, 17323;   **1598**: 12099;
1599: 25089;   **1600**: 6523, 6798, 21466;   **1601**: 18893, 18894,
19343;   **1602**: 26026;   **1603**: 14377;   **1604**: 17429;   **1605**: 17857,
18288;   **1607**: 710, 21461.
BLACK LETTER 2. 20ll.=54mm.   **1595**: [4042];   **1596**: [15281].
BLACK LETTER 3. 20ll.=67mm.   **1595**: 12161;   **1596**: [720],
[20797].

2. DEVICES AND COMPARTMENTS

On his title-pages, Simmes used eleven of the devices listed in
McKerrow,[2] and three of the compartments listed in McKerrow &
Ferguson.[3] The McKerrow devices are:

142.   **1596**: 17126.1;   **1597**: 17906, 22307, 22314;   **1598**: 3216, 22308;
1599: 4987;   **1600**: 3675, 3679, 6523, 18795, 21466, 26100;   **1601**: 18893,
18894, 20167;   **1602**: 1556, 6336;   **1603**: 7084, 7085, 21467;   **1604**: 343,
12058, 17429, 26040;   **1605**: 13875;   **1606**: 20983. McKerrow's account of
the history of this ornament is substantially correct, although sketchy.
Rowland Hall used it probably in 1562 in STC 11408, again in 1563 in
the book cited by McKerrow, and then it passed to William How. I can
find nothing to support McKerrow's suggestion that it may have passed
by way of Richard Serle. How's use of the device extended at least to
1587 where it is found in STC 12926. It passed to Simmes by 1596,
probably fairly close to that date (see discussion of Simmes's relations
with How below). It was used by Simmes regularly until 1606, when
it disappeared; Henry Ballard used it in 1608 again in one book (STC
17888).

261.   **1594**: 22860.   This device is assigned by McKerrow to Gregory
Seton, for whom Simmes printed this book.

289.   **1597**: 17323;   **1598**: 12099.   This device belonged to John Oxenbridge, for whom Simmes printed both books.

301.   **1601**: 22736;   **1602**: 26026;   **1603**: 22275;   **1605**: 7216;   **1607**: 6785,
23669. Nicholas Ling owned this rebus, and had used it since 1595.
All of these books were printed for Ling.

303.   **1595**: 3012;   **1596**: 1053, 15281, 19180.   McKerrow finds this

2. *Printers' and Publishers' Devices 1485-
1640.* (1949). This standard work will
hereafter be referred to as 'McKerrow.'

3. *Title-Page Borders used in England
and Scotland 1485-1640.* (1932). This work
will hereafter be referred to as 'McKerrow
& Ferguson.'

device used only by Simmes, and concludes that he owned it. It was certainly infrequently used, and was unsuitable because of its small size.

313.   **1600**: 11578; **1601**: 20053; **1602**: 20151; **1604**: 17429. This device belonged to Thomas Bushell, for whom the books were printed.

331.   **1601**: 25226; **1603**: 14377.   McKerrow suggests that this device may have belonged to William Wood. It was used in 1603 on STC 14377 which Simmes printed for John Harrison. The device may have passed to Harrison from White, who ceased publishing in 1601, or it may have been in Simmes's possession and used on these two books.

332.   **1597**: 24097; **1598**: 21311; **1599**: 25224; **1601**: 25765; **1602**: 2771, 24004; **1603**: 7539, 25221.   Simmes apparently owned this device, and in most cases it appeared on books he published for himself. McKerrow suggests that it passed to Kingston about 1608, which coincides with Simmes's replacement as a printer.

333.   **1602**: 17621.   This device is assigned by McKerrow to Simmes, and appears on this book which he published himself. McKerrow also records it on a title-page in the British Museum's collection.

341.   **1605**: 22766.   This book was printed for William Leake, to whom McKerrow assigns the device.

379.   **1599**: 25089; **1600**: 3675, 22288, 22304, 24152; **1601**: 19343, 26039; **1602**: 6373; **1603**: 3068, 5121, 13848; **1604**: 2811; **1605**: 702.1, 7216, 21717; **1606**: 13509; **1607**: 344, 6930, 15540. There were several copies of this ornament being used from 1583 to 1644. McKerrow suggests that it was a cast ornament, and the number of identical specimens seems to strengthen his suggestion. The different copies of this ornament, together with their owners, dates, and books, are as follows:

>Robert Waldegrave (?):   **1583**(?): 10394.
>(for) Thomas Cadman: **1587**(?): 25349.
>John Windet: **1587**: 5003; **1607**: 6241.
>Thomas Orwin: **1588**: 12803.
>John Wolfe: **1591**: 4864; **1601**: 23475.
>John Legatt: **1595**: Camb. Syn. 7.60.29^3 (not in STC); **1598**: 3088; **1617**: 19716.
>Peter Short: **1599**: 22358.
>R. Schilders: **1610**: 11134.

In addition to these, there are further uses by Andreas Hart of Edinburgh not noted by McKerrow. These were: **1620**: 21256; **1621**: 23660; **1631**: 21257.

None of these is the Simmes ornament (Fig. 2), which can be identified by the damage done to the right side of it (A), by the nick in the lower left (B), and, after 1605, by another nick in the right-hand moustache (C).

This ornament did not disappear when Simmes went out of business after 1607, but passed to Henry Ballard, and appeared that same year in Ballard's edition of *Gods Arrows* (STC 25057). He used it the next year in two books, STC 6357 and 7493.

Fig. 2
(2 x original size)

The following compartments from McKerrow & Ferguson's catalogue were used by Simmes:

147b.   **1600**: 6798.

229.   **1601**: 6236, 6237; **1602**: 1556 (sides only): **1603**: 6258, 6259.
These were Daniel folios. 18041.

235.   **1604**: 2811.

3.   ORNAMENTAL PIECES

Simmes's stock of ornaments consisted of a few dozen pieces of differing ages and popularity. Where many of them came from is not yet known, although it is known that some of his ornaments were acquired from Abel Jeffes.[4] His largest single known source was the acquisition of a large portion of the ornamental stock owned by William How. It consisted of four ornaments, sixteen initials, and one device (McKerrow 142). Two of these pieces (McKerrow 142 and Ornament 22) can be traced back through How to Roland Hall. Some of the pieces can be found in books How printed in the 70's, while others appear first in books he printed in the late 80's. Several can be seen in two of How's later publications, STC 11383 (1588) and 5721 (1590). Most of the ornaments obtained from How were used first in

4. This information was obtained from   Mr. K. T. Taylor of Oxford, who was
engaged in a study of Jeffes.

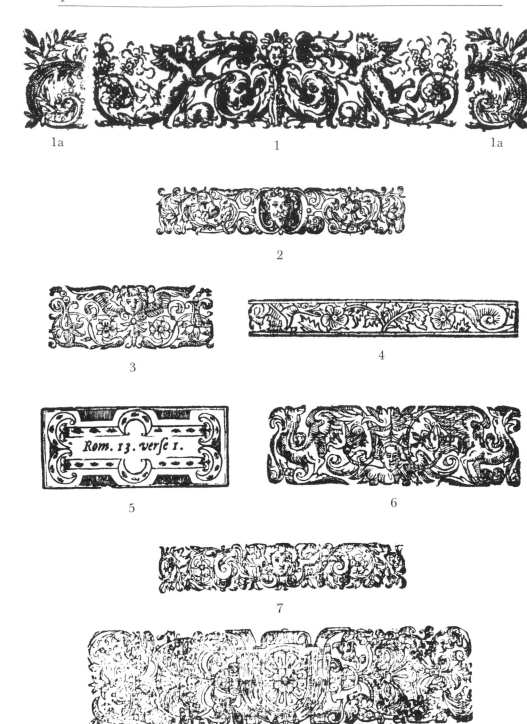

1a   1   1a

2

3

4

Rom. 13. verſe I.

5

6

7

8

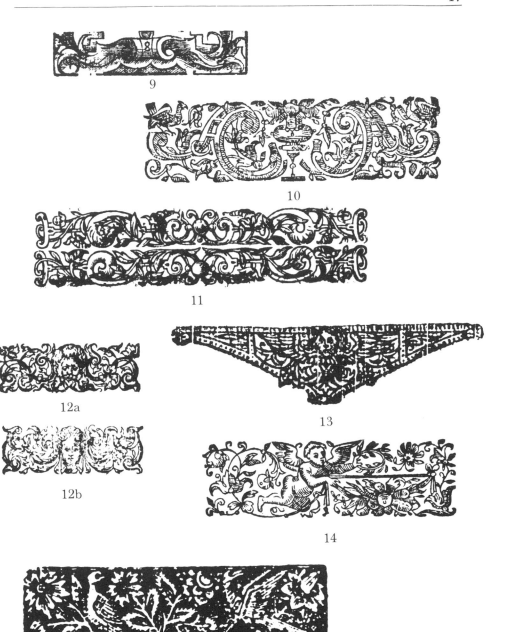

9

10

11

12a

13

12b

14

15

16

17

18

19

20

21

22

23

24

25

26

McK. 142

McK. 332

McK. 379

Flower 1

Flower 2

Flower 3

Flower 4

Flower 5

Flower 6

1595 or 1596. None appeared in 1594, suggesting that Simmes obtained the pieces from How very shortly before he began using them.

William How by this time was a senior stationer, retired from active printing, but still sitting as a member of the Court. The only positive link between him and Simmes is the fact that he is listed as one of the nine members of the Court which, on March 1, 1596, gave Simmes the right to print some of Bynneman's copies. One notes, in passing, that How did not sit on the Court the previous September when Simmes's type was ordered destroyed.

It is easier to trace some of Simmes's stock after it left his hands, for much of it appears in books printed by Henry Ballard. Ballard seems to have acquired some of Simmes's stock as early as 1607, when no less than four Simmes ornaments and a device (379) appear in one book (STC 25057).

The pieces are listed below according to the numbers assigned to them in this study, and are accompanied by a list of STC books in which they appear. These are followed by special pieces and leaf ornaments which are not numbered.

1. **1603**: 6258, 6259, 7084, 7085, 18041; **1604**: 94, 343, 26040; **1605**: 3058, 6071, 6457, 15448, 21717; **1606**: 5348.

1a. **1603**: 20170; **1604**: 94, 6501, 17479, 17480, 17481; **1605**: 1457, 1597, 3058, 6502; **1606**: 4978, 5348; **1607**: 344. This ornament originally measured 26 x 129mm., but the two ends had been cut off and used as separate ornaments. The central piece, referred to as ornament 1, measures 26 x 96mm.; the two end pieces, ornament 1a, measure 26 x 16mm. and 26 x 16mm. Occasionally all three pieces are found together, but usually they were used as two ornaments. The two end pieces were often used as title-page ornaments, sometimes standing on end, sometimes on their sides, but always used together. Ornament 1 passed to Henry Ballard.[5]

2. **1596**: 182; **1600**: 6798, 11578; **1601**: 20053, 20167, 25226; **1602**: 24004; **1604**: 2811.   12 x 67mm. This was a fairly common design; Dr. C. William Miller[6] illustrates a larger ornament of basically the same design.

3. **1597**: 22314; **1601**: 20053, 25765, 26039; **1604**: 14756.   18 x 45.5mm. Simmes acquired this ornament from Abel Jeffes, who used it in

5. Mr John Cook Wyllie, in private correspondence, has noted that George Eld had an ornament similar to 1a which he was using around 1606. It can be distinguished from Simmes's copy by a different arrangement of leaves around the outer edges. Mr Wyllie has noted too a cutting of the main ornament in the stock of Andro Hart in Edinburgh, 1620 (STC 17616).

6. "A London Ornament Stock: 1598-1683." *Studies in Bibliography, Vol. VII*, p. 141. This work will be referred to hereafter as 'Miller.'

1595 in his *World of Wonders* (not in STC). It is found also on the title-page of a book printed ostensibly by Simon Stafford for William Barley: STC 3696 (1598). See discussion above, p. 17.

4. **1604**: 2811. 10 x 77mm. Obtained from William How.

5. **1596**: 1829; **1601**: 20053, 25765; **1603**: 3068, 13848. 22 x 50mm. This too was obtained from How, who used it vertically as a factotum, while Simmes used it as a demi-compartment. It passed to Ballard.

6. **1597**: 22314; **1598**: 3216, 16667, 17760; **1601**: 25226; **1602**: 24004. 21 x 68mm. This ornament was acquired from Jeffes.

7. **1595**: 7299; **1597**: 24097; **1598**: 3216, 16667; **1599**: 18370; **1601**: 20053, 25226; **1602**: 24004; **1604**: 2811. 12 x 66mm. This ornament is mentioned in Miller (number 16) as having belonged to Judson, and appearing in STC 18370. This book was printed by Judson and Simmes, and the ornament appears in the section of the book printed by Simmes.

8. **1595**: 4101, 22971; **1596**: 1829, 20797, 22972; **1598**: 3216, 10253, 16667; **1600**: 6798; **1601**: 6236, 6237; **1603**: 6259, 18041; **1605**: 3058. 25 x 104mm.

9. **1598**: 3216; **1602**: 2771, 17621, 24004; **1603**: 7539. 12 x 53.5mm. Belonged to Jeffes until 1596. Judging by the cracks which appear in the Bodleian copy of STC 24004, this was probably a woodcut.

10. **1597**: 17323, 17906, 22307, 22314; **1598**: 3696, 16667, 17760, 21311; **1599**: 4987, 18370, 26019; **1600**: 3675, 3679, 18795, 21466, 22288, 26100; **1601**: 19343, 20167; **1602**: 5347; **1603**: 5121, 20170, 21467, 22275; **1604**: 343, 20889, 22282; **1605**: 1457, 1597, 7216; **1606**: 4978, 20983; **1607**: 6930, 21461. 21 x 77mm. One of Simmes's most popular ornaments, this was obtained from the Jeffes stock after 1595. Miller includes this in his list (number 14) and again assigns it to Judson in STC 18370. Again, the ornament appeared in the Simmes section of the book. It passed to Ballard by 1608.

11. **1600**: 3675, 3679, 6523, 6798, 18795, 21466, 22304, 26100; **1601**: 6236, 6237, 18893, 18894, 20053, 20167, 25226; **1602**: 1556, 5347, 6336, 26026; **1603**: 5121, 7084, 7085, 15355, 20170; **1604**: 6501, 17429, 17479, 17480, 17481; **1605**: 6502; **1606**: 5348; **1607**: 344, 11842, 15535, 15540. 10 x 89mm. Simmes used at least three of these ornaments, often to decorate the top and bottom of a page of verse. They were acquired by Ballard.

12.(a and b) **1594**: 22860; **1595**: 3012, 23361; **1596**: 20797; **1601**: 26039. 26039.

12a. **1595**: 7299; **1598**: 12099.

12b. **1600**: 20150.   Each piece measures 13 x 36.5mm. These complementary ornaments were usually used together, and in only three books was one used without the other. They were popular with Simmes during the early years of his career, and 12a turns up in Ballard's stock in 1609.

13. **1597**: 15379.   21 x 83mm. This tailpiece appears only once in the Simmes section of a shared book, and may have been borrowed.

14. **1598**: 21311; **1599**: 17994; **1601**: 25226; **1602**: 2771, 17621, 24004. 21 x 68mm. This ornament appears in 1613 in STC 15433, printed by Ralph Blower.

15. **1598**: 12099.   15 x 60mm. This appears to be an old woodcut.

16. **1598**: 22308; **1599**: 26019; **1600**: 3679; **1603**: 20170; **1605**: 13857; **1606**: 13509; **1607**: 710, 23669.   15 x 82mm.

17. **1599**: 25089; **1600**: 6523, 22304; **1601**: 6236, 6237, 20167; **1602**: 1556, 26026; **1603**: 20170; **1605**: 20753; **1607**: 15535.   40 x 88mm. inside measure, outside measure 21 to 60 mm. This demi-compartment is of the same general design as ornament 11, and, in all except its first appearance, is used in the same books as number 11, apparently in an attempt to unify the styles of the ornaments used.

18. **1599**: 18370.   16 x 68mm. This is the only time Simmes used this ornament, and it appears in his stint of the book shared with Judson. Miller lists this as number 13 in his study, and assigns it to Judson on the basis of another book. It is possible that Simmes did borrow this ornament from Judson for this book.

19. **1602**: 6373; **1604**: 2811, 26040; **1605**: 6071, 6457, 13857, 22766; **1606**: 4978; **1607**: 15535, 15540. Each section measures 3 x 17mm. It was used primarily as a border or a rule. It appears later in books by both Ballard and Blower.

20. **1603**: 5121; **1605**: 6071.   58 x 57mm. This appears in Miller as number 31. It appears to be a cast, and there is no reason to believe that there was only one copy.

21. **1605**: 6071.   51 x 45mm. Miller number 32. This appears also to be a cast, and is similar in design to 20.

22. **1595**: 22971; **1596**: 182, 17126.1; **1597**: 17323, 22307; **1599**: 17994; **1600**: 3679, 6798, 11578; **1601**: 19343; **1603**: 5121, 14377, 16676; **1604**: 2811, 20889.   29 x 57mm. This is an old piece, probably of wood, which was used by Rowland Hall in 1564 in STC 432, and by an unidentified printer in 1565 in STC 15220. It passed then to How and from him to Simmes.

23.   **1598**: 10253; **1603**: 15355; **1604**: 94; **1606**: 13509; **1607**: 6785, 23669.   38 x 48mm.

24.   **1601**: 6236.   14 x 48mm. Simmes had at least two such pieces, as illustrated.

25.   **1601**: 6236, 6237.   36 x 40mm.

26.   **1604**: 17481.   18 x 89mm. Obtained from How.

Lion.   **1596**: 23362; **1600**: 11578.   52 x 32mm.

Royal Arms, 'ER'.   **1595**: 3012, 23361; **1596**: 23362.   51 x 36mm. (not illustrated)

Royal Arms, 'Semper Eadem'.   **1601**: 6236, 6237.   43 x 121mm. Used in the same book as McKerrow & Ferguson 229, which bears the same motto. (not illustrated)

THE.   **1603**: 18041; **1604**: 94, 6501, 17479, 17480, 17481; **1605**: 6457, 6402, 13857; **1606**: 4978; **1607**: 710, 13317, 21461.   20 x 75mm. This word is a solid block, used on title-pages. Sir Walter Greg notes it,[7] and describes two similar blocks which appeared in 1607.

FLOWER 1.   **1594**: 709, 22860; **1595**: 3012, 3314, 4101, 4102, 12161, 15638, 22954, 23361; **1596**: 182, 720, 1053, 1828, 1829, 14802, 15281, 19180, 20797, 22972, 23362; **1597**: 15379, 17906, 22314, 24097; **1598**: 1047, 3216, 21311; **1599**: 4987, 17994, 25224, 26019; **1600**: 3679, 11578, 24152; **1601**: 22736, 25226; **1602**: 2771, 6373, 17621, 24004; **1603**: 3068, 5121, 6258, 6259, 7539, 13592, 14377, 18041; **1604**: 94, 343, 2811, 14756, 20889, 22282; **1605**: 702.1, 1457, 3058, 7216, 13857, 15448, 22766; **1606**: 5348, 13509, 14774: **1607**: 344, 710, 6785, 11842, 15535, 15540, 21461.   Each segment measures 6 x 6mm. This was Simmes's most popular flower, and was used for borders, rules, and title-page ornaments in almost half his books. It is a cast ornament, and Simmes had many of them. This flower is often seen elsewhere in the 16th Century, and the illustration of McKerrow 220 shows how Christopher Barker tastefully employed it in 1579. See the discussion by Francis Meynell and Stanley Morison: "Printers' Flowers and Arabesques." *The Fleuron*, No. 1 (1923). Ballard seems to have acquired Simmes's stock of the ornament.

FLOWER 2.   **1594**: 709; **1595**; 3012, 3314, 4042, 4101, 4102, 22954; **1596**: 182, 720, 1053, 1828, 1829, 13252, 14802, 15281, 17126.1, 19180, 20797, 22972, 23362; **1597**: 15379, 17906, 24097; **1598**: 3216, 21311; **1599**: 17994, 18370, 25224, 26019; **1600**: 3675, 3679, 6253, 11578; **1601**: 19343, 25765; **1602**: 6386, 20151, 24004; **1603**: 6258, 6250, 13828, 14377, 18041; **1604**: 94, 343, 22282; **1605**: 702.1, 3058, 7216, 13857, 15448, 18288, 22766; **1606**: 5348, 13509; **1607**:

7.   *A Bibliography of the English Printed   Drama to the Restoration.* (1939). Vol. 1, p. 322.

11842, 15535, 15540. Each segment measures 6 x 6mm. This flower was almost as popular as flower 1. The two flowers were often used together, and sometimes, by combining them, Simmes was able to achieve title-page ornaments like the one shown at the end of the illustrations. The judicious use of both ornaments is a characteristic of Simmes's work. It too went to Ballard.

FLOWER. 3. **1594:** 709; **1595:** 4101, 10418, 23361; **1596:** 13252; **1597:** 22314; **1606:** 14774; **1607:** 344, 11842, 15535, 21461. Each segment, 5.5 x 5.5mm.

FLOWER 4. **1595:** 3314, 4101, 12161; **1596:** 1828, 13252, 14802, 15281, 17126.1; **1597:** 15379, 17323, 24097; **1599:** 4987, 17994; **1600:** 6798; **1602:** 24004, 26026; **1603:** 14377, **1604:** 6501, 14756; **1605:** 1597, 7216; **1606:** 5348; **1607:** 710, 6785, 15535, 15540, 23669. This small, conventional leaf was used to set off important sentences or lines of type.

FLOWER 5. **1595:** 22971; **1596:** 17126.1, 22972; **1597:** 17906; **1598:** 21311. Each segment, 6 x 7.5mm. A rather ugly ornament, used early in Simmes's career, and out of character with the arabesque designs.

FLOWER 6. **1601:** 6236, 6237; **1605:** 3058, 6071. Each segment, 6 x 9mm.

FLOWER 7. **1611:** 14646, 15227. 5 x 6.5mm. This may or may not have belonged to Simmes, being used in two books at the end of his career. (not illustrated)

FLOWER 8. **1611:** 14646. This, like leaf 7, may have been borrowed. It measures only 3 x 5mm. (not illustrated)

4. FACTOTUMS

Most printers of this period had several factotums, but Simmes had only three, and they appear to be unique, forming a fairly sound basis for identifying a Simmes book.

FACT. 1. **1594:** 709, 22860; **1595:** 3314, 4101, 4102, 22964, 23361; **1596:** 720, 1829, 15281, 17126.1, 19180, 20797, 22972; **1597:** 15379, 17323, 17906; **1598:** 1047, 3216, 21311; **1599:** 26019; **1600:** 6798, 11578, 21466; **1601:** 18894, 20053, 22736, 25765; **1602:** 1556, 2771, 24004, 26026; **1603:** 7084, 7085, 18041, 20170; **1604:** 94, 17481, 20889, 26040; **1605:** 1457, 6457, 13857, 15448, 20753a; **1606:** 5348, 13509; **1607:** 11842, 15540, 21461. 32 x 32mm. This was Simmes's favorite factotum, and appears in a third of his books. The facto-

Logotype

Factotum 1

Factotum 2

Lion

Factotum 3

A1

A2

A3

A4

A5

B1

B2

B3

B4

B5

B6

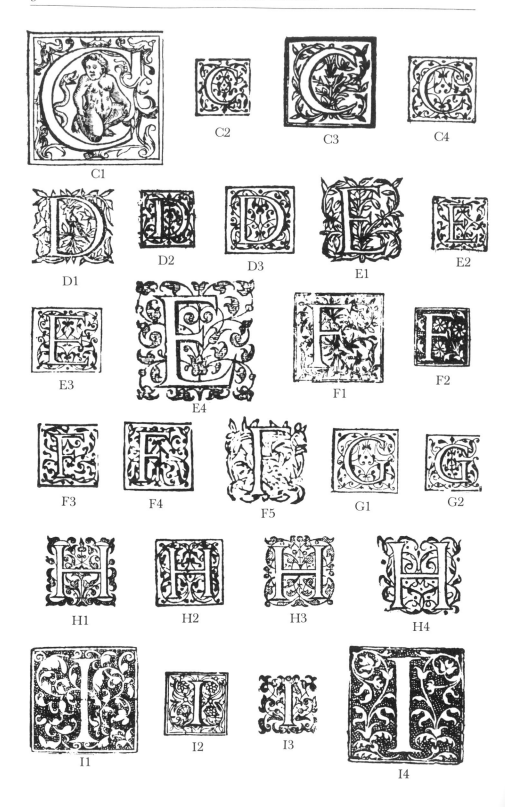

C1

C2

C3

C4

D1

D2

D3

E1

E2

E3

E4

F1

F2

F3

F4

F5

G1

G2

H1

H2

H3

H4

I1

I2

I3

I4

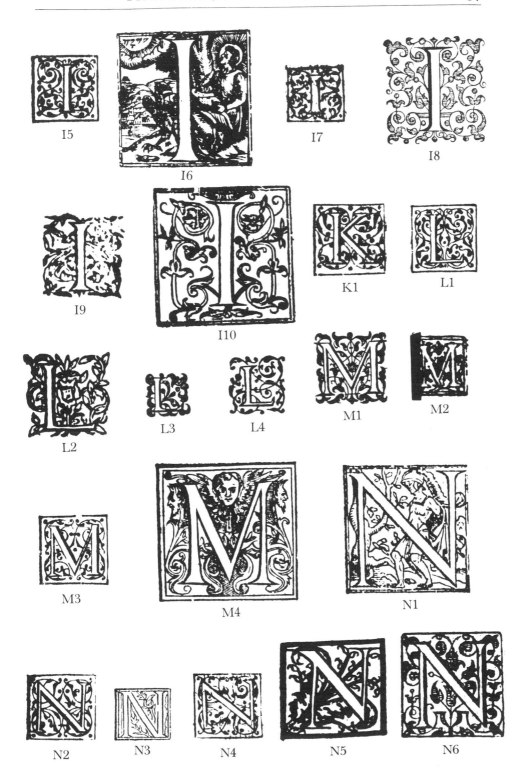

I5

I6

I7

I8

I9

I10

K1

L1

L2

L3

L4

M1

M2

M3

M4

N1

N2

N3

N4

N5

N6

N7   N8   O1   O2   O3

O4   P1   P2   Q1

R1   R2   R3   S1   S2

S3   S4   S5

T1   T2   T3   T4   T5

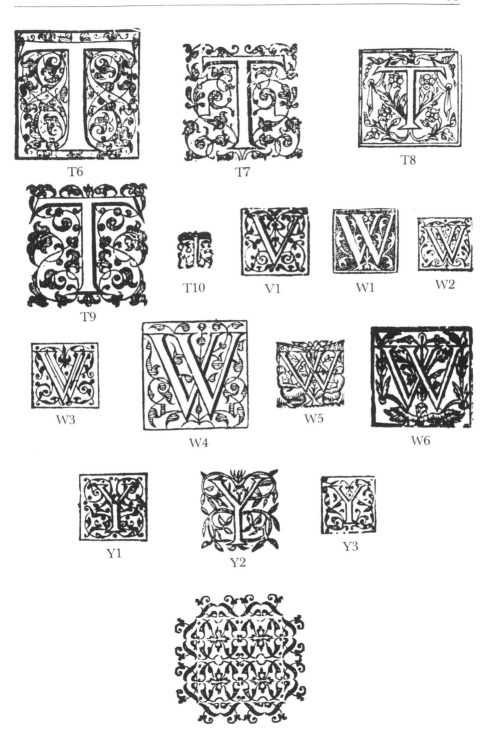

T6

T7

T8

T9

T10

V1

W1

W2

W3

W4

W5

W6

Y1

Y2

Y3

tum appears also in the book Simmes and Blower set together in 1612, STC 17844. However, it now has rules around it. Blower used it again that year in STC 23608, and in 1613 in STC 15433.

FACT. 2.   **1595**: 4042, 7299, 23361; **1596**: 720, 19180, 23362; **1597**: 15379; **1598**: 21311; **1600**: 18795, 20150, 26100; **1601**: 6236, 6237, 260039; **1602**: 6373, 20151, 24004; **1603**: 3068, 20170; **1604**: 343, 26040; **1605**: 6457; **1607**: 344, 6930, 13317, 15540.   21 x 21mm. There were factotums similar to this in use at the same time; Creede had one, but they are not exactly the same in design. This piece went to Ballard in 1607, and appeared in STC 25057.

FACT. 3.   **1598**: 21311; **1599**: 18370; **1600**: 3675, 6798; **1601**: 6236, 6237, 18893; **1603**: 5121, 6259, 18041, 21467; **1604**: 94, **1605**: 1457, 1597, 15448, 18288, 21717; **1607**: 6785.   44 x 45mm. This factotum is listed in Miller, number 1. Again, he is quoting only one book, STC 18370, printed by Simmes and Judson. Again, the piece is found only in the Simmes section of the book. During 1605 a break appeared in the top (or bottom, depending on use) line of the factotum.

5.   DECORATIVE INITIALS

Simmes had an adequate stock of decorative initials. It was a miscellaneous collection, without any attempt at standardizing design patterns or size. Some initials are obviously older than others, some follow conventional designs and are seen in the works of other printers. The initials and their occurrences are listed below.

A-1.   **1595**: 23361; **1596**: 182, 15281; **1597**: 15379; **1599**: 25224; **1602**: 17621; **1604**: 20889, 26040; **1605**: 20753. 21 x 21mm. Peter Short used a similar initial in *Palladis tamia* (STC 17834, **1598**).

A-2.   **1596**: 15281, 17126.1; **1597**: 15379, 17323; **1604**: 26040.   21 x 22 mm.

A-3.   **1596**: 15281, 29797; **1599**: 26019.   37 x 37mm. This would appear by the initials to have belonged to a printer with the initials 'I.R.' Isaac's discussion of Nicholas Hill and John Reynes[8] suggests that the initial may have belonged originally to the latter. He notes that Reynes' initials are found in the books of several later printers, including Simmes and Kingston. This initial appears in Kingston's work (STC 17164) and a similar initial, also bearing the 'IR' signature, is found in the work of Nicholas Hill (STC 19493, sig. C7.)

8. In his *English Printers' Types of the Sixteenth Century*, p. 24f.

A-4. **1596:** 17126.1 **1598:** 24477; **1602:** 26026; **1604:** 26040; **1605:** 22766; **1606:** 20983. 21 x 22mm.

A-5. **1595:** 10418; **1597;** 17906; **1599:** 12273; **1600:** 3679, 11578; **1601:** 26039; **1602:** 20151; **1604:** 2811, 26040. 14 x 14mm. The bottom line appears unbroken in 1595. Obtained from How.

B-1. **1595:** 3314; **1599;** 26019; **1601:** 22736; **1607:** 710. 29 x 30mm. This initial appears to be old, and probably represents the Last Supper.

B-2. **1597:** 17323. 17 x 18mm.

B-3. **1595:** 22955; **1596:** 15281; **1599:** 26019; **1601:** 26039, 6236, 6237; **1602:** 17621. 18 x 18mm. From How.

B-4. **1596:** 1828. 29 x 28mm.

B-5. **1603:** 18041. 29 x 30mm. Satyr blowing pipe.

B-6. **1597:** 15379; **1607:** 12255. 22 x 22mm.

C-1. **1595:** 4101. 35 x 36mm. Roberts had a copy of this initial, which is distinguishable from Simmes's. Roberts used it in 1594 in STC 11622.

C-2. **1597:** 17906; **1599:** 11578; **1603:** 5121. 15 x 15mm. Obtained from How; passed to Ballard.

C-3. **1601:** 25765; **1603:** 3068; **1604:** 20889. 24 x 23.5mm.

C-4. **1596:** 15281. 18 x 18mm.

D-1. **1597:** 15379; **1607:** 6930. 21 x 23mm.

D-2. **1598:** 24477. 16 x 16mm. From How

D-3. **1604:** 343; **1606:** 13509. 17 x 17mm.

E-1. **1596:** 13252, 15281, 17126.1. 22 x 22mm.

E-2. **1595:** 7299; **1596:** 15281; **1599:** 25224. 14 x 15mm. From How

E-3. **1596:** 15281. 17 x 19mm.

E-4. **1604:** 94. 31.5 x 31mm. Miller finds this initial used by Wilson in 1655.

F-1. **1596:** 15281; **1604:** 94. 24 x 24mm.

F-2. **1595:** 12161; **1597:** 24097. 16 x 15mm.

F-3. **1599:** 25224; **1600:** 11578; **1601:** 6236, 6237, 26039; **1603:** 18041; **1605:** 702.1. 15 x 15mm.

F-4. **1595:** 10418; **1602:** 17621; **1604:** 26040. 18 x 18mm.

F-5. **1595:** 10418; **1604:** 26040.

G-1. **1595:** 7299; **1597:** 749, 15379, 24097; **1598:** 16667; **1606:** 10456. 17 x 18mm. Passed to Ballard.

G-1. **1595:** 7299; **1597:** 749, 15379, 24097; **1598:** 16667; **1606:** 10456. 17 x 18mm. Passed to Ballard.

H-1. **1594:** 709; **1595:** 3314, 4042; **1598:** 24477; **1603:** 7539; **1606:** 5348. 18 x 19mm.

H-2.   **1596**: 13252; **1597**: 15379; **1598**: 3216; **1600**: 3679; **1606**: 4978, 10456.   17.5 x 18mm.

H-3.   **1595**: 3012, 23361; **1601**: 6236, 6237; **1602**: 6336, 17621; **1603**: 6258, 6259; **1604**: 26040; **1607**: 710.   19 x 19mm. Passed to Ballard.

H-4.   **1597**: 15379.   21 x 23mm.

I-1.   **1595**: 3314.   29 x 29mm.

I-2.   **1595**: 3314, 12161, 22954, 23361; **1596**: 19180; **1597**: 15379, 17323, 17906.   17 x 17mm. From How.

I-3.   **1595**: 3012, 15638, 22971; **1597**: 17323; **1598**: 3216, 21311; **1599**: 25224; **1600**: 11578, 20150, 22304; **1601**: 6236, 6237, 26039; **1602**: 2771, 24004; **1603**: 7539, 18041; **1604**: 2811, 17481, 26040.   16 x 15mm.

I-4.   **1596**: 15281; **1601**: 20167 **1602**: 26026; **1604**: 26040.   31 x 31mm.

I-5.   **1596**: 13252, 22972; **1597**: 17323; **1602**: 17621; **1603**: 7539, 14377; **1605**: 15448.   18 x 18mm. From How.

I-6.   **1597**: 17323; **1598**: 12099, 21311; **1601**: 19343, 25765; **1603**: 13848; **1605**: 15448, 22766.   35 x 36mm. From How. Robert Barker used an initial of this design in 1604 (STC 14390).

I-7.   **1596**: 19180; **1597**: 17323, 17906; **1598**: 24477; **1602**: 17621; **1605**: 6457.   14 x 15mm. From How.

I-8.   **1606**: 5348; **1607**: 6930.   28 x 27mm.

I-9.   **1595**: 10418; **1607**: 6930.   22 x 22mm. Obtained from How; passed to Ballard.

I-10:   **1602**: 5347; **1604**: 17479, 17480; **1605**: 1457, 20753, 20753a; **1606**: 14774.   36 x 37mm.

K-1.   **1599**: 25224; **1600**: 6253.   18 x 18mm.

L-1.   **1596**: 720, 23362.   17.5 x 17.5mm.

L-2.   **1595**: 23361; **1597**: 17323.   21 x 22mm.

L-3.   **1595**: 23361; **1598**: 3216; **1603**: 20170; **1604**: 343.   11 x 12mm.

L-4.   **1601**: 6236, 6237, 26039, **1603**: 6258, 6259.   15 x 15mm.

M-1.   **1595**: 3012, 15638, 22972; **1596**: 182; **1600**: 6523, 18795, 21466; **1601**: 6236, 6237; **1602**: 20151; **1603**: 6259, 13592, 18041; **1605**: 3058, 15448.   19 x 18mm.

M-2.   **1600**: 11578.   15 x 14mm.

M-3.   **1599**: 25224; **1600**: 3679; **1603**: 21467.   17.5 x 18mm.

M-4.   **1595**: 23361.   35 x 35mm. This initial may have been borrowed for the specific purpose of opening a religious book.

N-1.   **1596**: 17126.1, 20797; **1599**: 18370; **1604**: 26040.   33 x 33mm. Miller assigns this initial to Judson, but again it is in the Simmes portion of the book they shared.

N-2. **1596**: 182; **1601**: 26039. 17.5 x 18mm. Obtained from How; passed to Ballard.

N-3. **1597**: 749, 22314. 15 x 16mm.

N-4. **1598**: 24477, 17760. 19 x 20mm. This could be a turned 'Z'.

N-5. **1603**: 18041. 27 x 28mm.

N-6. **1599**: 26019; **1601**: 22736; **1603**: 20170. 28.5 x 27mm.

N-7. **1601**: 26039; **1603**: 13848; **1607**: 6930, 12255. 17.5 x 17mm.

N-8. **1604**: 26040; **1605**: 7299. 14.5 x 14.5mm.

O-1. **1595**: 3012, 4042; **1598**: 22308; **1599**: 26019; **1600**: 22288. 18 x 18mm.

O-2. **1595**: 3012, 4042, 22954; **1597**: 17906, 22307; **1600**: 11578; **1601**: 6236, 6237, 26039; **1603**: 18041. 15 x 15mm. Passed to Ballard.

O-3. **1596**: 15281; **1597**: 15379. 22 x 22mm.

O-4. **1595**: 3012; **1596**: 15281. 21 x 21mm. Passed to Ballard.

O-5. **1595**: 3012. 17.5 x 18mm. (Not illustrated)

P-1. **1595**: 7299, 22954; **1596**: 13252; **1600**: 3679; **1603**: 6258, 6259; **1604**: 2811, 14756. 17 x 18mm.

P-2. **1596**: 15281. 21 x 22mm.

Q1. **1596**: 15281. 21 x 22mm.

R-1. **1595**: 22954; **1600**: 20150; **1601**: 20053. 15 x 15mm. Passed to Ballard.

R-2. ˙1596: 182, 15281; **1598**: 24477; **1605**: 20753a. 22 x 22mm. Passed to Ballard.

R-3. **1595**: 3012; **1598**: 12099; **1600**: 20150; **1602**: 17621, 20151, 24004; **1603**: 18041. 15 x 15mm. Passed to Ballard.

S-1. **1595**: 12161, 22954; **1596**: 15281, 17126.1; **1597**: 15379; **1598**: 16667; **1604**: 26040, 26840; **1607**: 12255. 17 x 18mm. From How.

S-2. **1596**: 15281; **1604**: 22282; **1607**: 12255. 21 x 22mm.

S-3. **1596**: 15281; **1605**: 1457; **1607**: 6930. 33 x 34mm. Miller notes that Okes was using an initial of this design in 1612.

S-4. **1595**: 3012; **1599**: 17994; **1601**: 26039; **1604**: 2811. 12 x 10mm. Passed to Ballard.

S-5. **1603**: 18041. 35 x 34mm.

T-1. **1594**: 709, 22860; **1595**: 3314; **1596**: 1053, 1828, 1829, 15281, 23362; **1599**: 26019; **1601**: 25765. 32 x 32mm.

T-2. **1595**: 3012, 4042; **1596**: 15281; **1600**: 11578; **1601**: 6236, 6237, 26039; **1602**: 2771, 6336, 17621, 20151; **1603**: 6258, 6259, 18041; **1605**: 6457; **1607**: 6785, 15535. 15 x 15mm. Passed to Ballard.

T-3. **1595**: 3314, 22954, 23361; **1596**: 13252, 23362; **1597**: 15379, 17323; **1600**: 11578; **1601**: 20167. 18 x 18mm. From How.

T-4. **1595**: 22954, 23361; **1597**: 15379, 17323; **1599**: 25224, 26019. 14 x 15mm. From How.

T-5.   **1595**: 12161, 23361; **1596**: 182, 17126.1, 19180; **1597**: 15379; **1604**: 26040; **1605**: 22766; **1607**: 6930, 11842.   18 x 18mm. Passed to Ballard.

T-6.   **1595**: 4101.   34 x 33mm.

T-7.   **1597**: 17906; **1598**: 16667, 21311.   31 x 32mm.

T-8.   **1598**: 16667, 21311; **1600**: 3679; **1601**: 25226; **1605**: 1457, 3058, 22766; **1607**: 6930.   26 x 27mm.

T-9.   **1603**: 6259, 18041; **1604**: 94, 26040; **1605**: 1457, 13857, 20753; **1606**: 5348; **1607**: 15535.   32 x 32mm.

T-10:   **1603**: 20170.   9 x 9mm.

V-1.   **1603**: 6258, 6259.   18 x 18mm.

W-1.   **1595**: 22954, 23361; **1597**: 15379; **1602**: 6336.   17 x 18mm.

W-2.   **1596**: 720; **1597**: 15379, 17906, 24097.   15 x 15mm. From How.

W-3.   **1596**: 720, 15281, 17126.1; **1597**: 15379, 17906; **1599**: 25089; **1600**: 3675, 3679; **1601**: 20167, 26039; **1602**: 20151; **1603**: 6258, 6259; **1604**: 343; **1605**: 7216; **1606**: 10456.   18 x 18mm. From How.

W-4.   **1605**: 6071, 18288.   28 x 27mm. This initial is also found in Creede's section of 15379. Miller finds it used by Norton in 1633. It appears to be a cast.

W-5.   **1607**: 6930.   18 x 19mm.

W-6.   **1601**: 25765; **1604**: 26040; **1606**: 13509; **1607**: 344.   26 x 26mm. Jeffes owned this initial until 1596.

W-7.   **1601**: 25765.   21 x 21mm.

Y-1.   **1597**: 17906; **1605**: 22766.   17.5 x 18mm.

Y-2.   **1605**: 22766; **1606**: 20983.   21 x 20.5mm. Passed to Ballard.

Y-3.   **1601**: 6236, 6237.   14 x 14mm.

6. Paper

The paper used by Simmes varied, but was usually of fairly good quality. Some books were printed on excellent paper, and very few on coarse paper. Occasionally a sheet of poor paper finds its way into a copy, where it is noticeable by the contrast with the remainder. Occasionally Simmes used a very good quality paper for presentation copies.

The watermarks vary enormously, and Allan H. Stevenson points out the dangers inherent in trying to identify watermarks, or in assuming that marks are identical.[7] A query beside an entry in this list

7. "Watermarks are Twins," *Studies in Bibliography, Vol. IV.* (1951). Here I must note that recent advances in beta-radiography have revolutionized the copying of watermarks, and rendered my copies obsolete. Realizing that they are, by comparison, poor things, I present them hoping they will be of some interest to the reader.

1-4

5-8

9-12

13-16

17-20

21-23

24-27

28-31

32-35

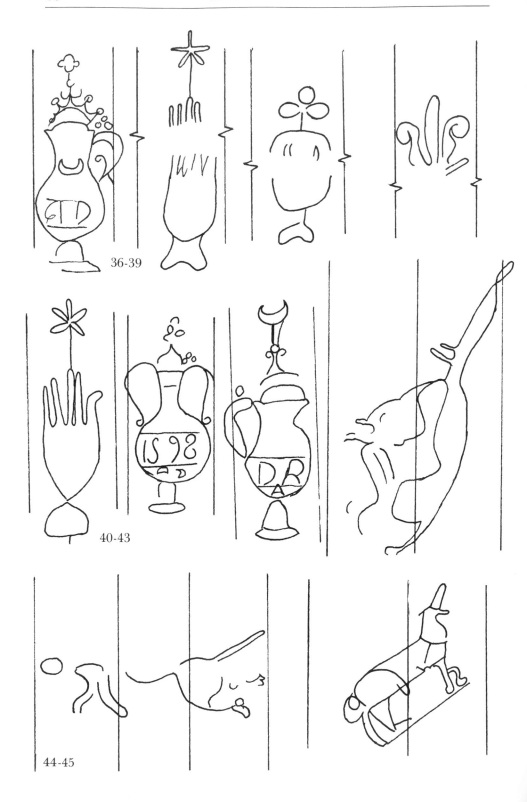

36-39

40-43

44-45

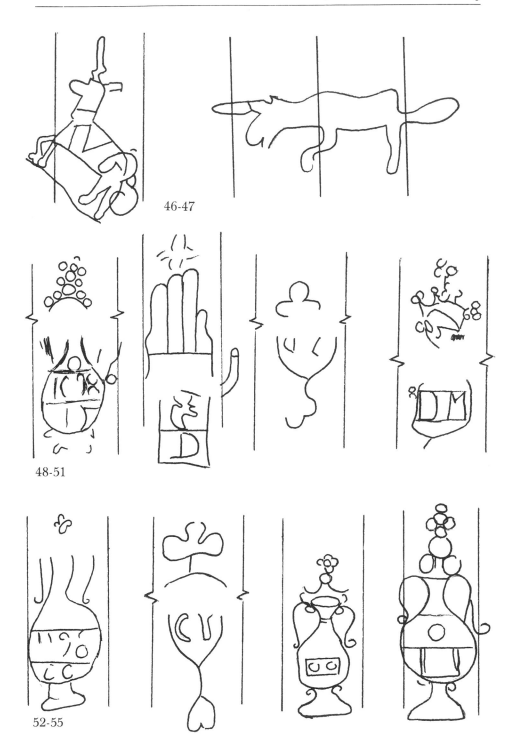

46-47

48-51

52-55

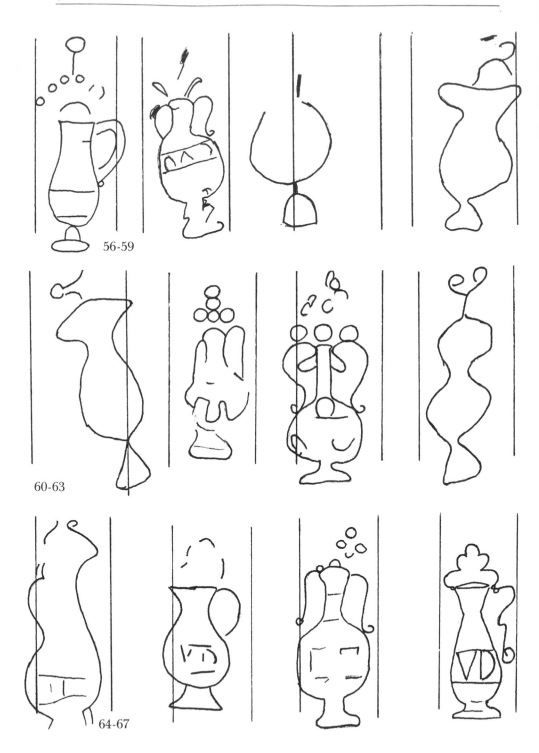

56-59

60-63

64-67

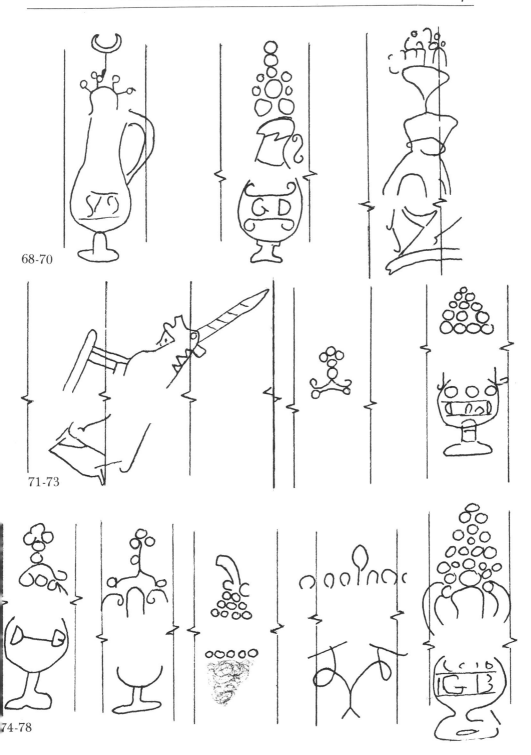

68-70

71-73

74-78

79-83

84-87

88-91

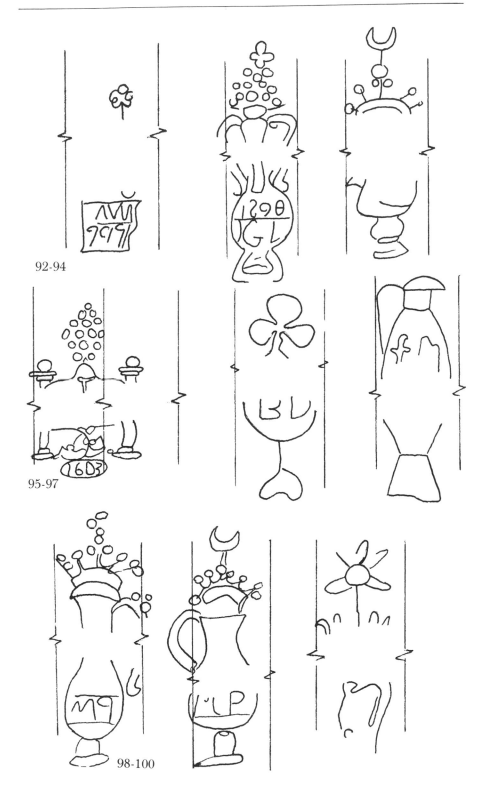

92-94

95-97

98-100

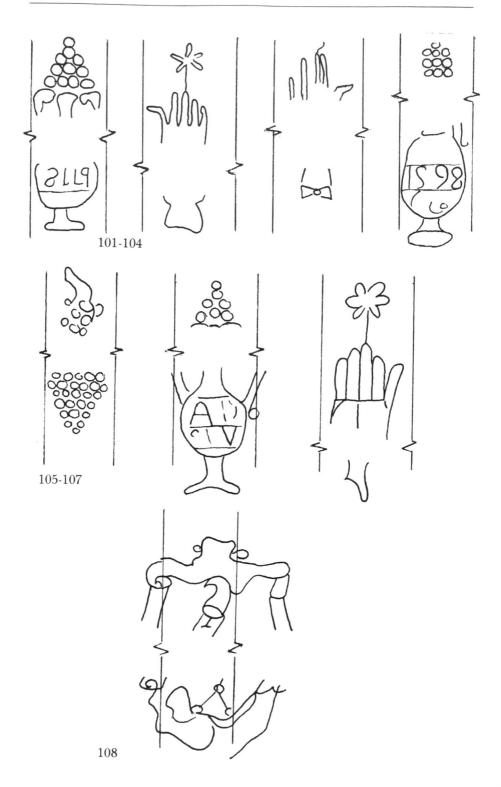

101-104

105-107

108

indicates that two marks seem identical, but that they may merely be similar, and that it would be dangerous to attempt a more positive identification.

In the following list, each of the 108 representative watermarks is numbered as in the illustrations, and is followed by the numbers of the STC books in which it occurs, and the distance between the chain-lines enclosing the mark. In many cases part of the mark is within the binding, and in the illustrations the break in the mark is indicated by a zig-zag mark on the chainlines.

1. **1594**: 709; **1595**: 4102; **1596**: 720.   22mm.
2. **1595**: 3314.   24.5mm.
3. **1595**: 4104.   23mm.
4. **1595**: 4102; **1596**: 15281(?).   23.5mm.
5. **1595**: 4102.   23mm.
6. **1595**: 4102.   21.5mm.
7. **1595**: 22954.   21mm.
8. **1595**: 22954.   22.5mm.
9. **1595**: 23361.   24, 23mm.
10. **1595**: 23361; **1596**: 720(?).   25mm.
11. **1596**: 720, 19180, 23362.   21mm.
12. **1596**: 720, 1829.   24mm.
13. **1596**: 720, 17126.1.   21mm.
14. **1596**: 720, 1829; **1597**: 15379.   26mm.
15. **1596**: 720, 1052, 13252(?).   23mm.
16. **1596**: 720.   22.5mm.
17. **1596**: 1828, 1829; **1597**: 15379, 17906, 22307, 22314; **1598**: 3216; **1599**: 26019; **1600**: 6523, 26100.   22mm.
18. **1597**: 17906, 22307, 22314; **1598**: 21311(?); **1600**: 24152(?). Variant initials, **1596**: 19180 (RE/N); **1599**: 4987 (PD/B).   23mm.
19. **1596**: 1829, 20797.   26mm.
20. **1596**: 20797; **1597**: 15379.   41mm. Compare Edward Heawood's mark 101.[8]
21. **1596**: 22972.   23, 22mm.
22. **1596**: 22972.   30mm. Heawood notes this curious design (164) and suggests that it is an English paper. The use of a Tudor emblem seems to indicate that he may be right.
23. **1596**: 23362.   24mm.
24. **1597**: 15379.   20mm.
25. **1597**: 17906; **1598**: 3216, 21311; **1600**: 6523, 26100(?).   21mm.
26. **1597**: 17906, 22314; **1598**: 21311; **1600**: 21466.   21.5mm.

8. "Sources of Early English Paper Supply." *The Library*, Vol. X, No. 4. p.431.

27. **1597**: 17906.   24mm.
28. **1597**: 22314; **1598**: 3216.   22mm.
29. **1598**: 12099.   21mm.
30. **1598**: 21311.   23.5mm.
31. **1599**: 4978.   21mm.
32. **1599**: 17994; **1600**: 18795(?).   21mm.
33. **1599**: 18370.   22mm.
34. **1600**: 3675.   26mm. (turned chains)
35. **1600**: 6523.   25mm.
36. **1600**: 6798, 26100; **1603**: 6258.   21mm.
37. **1600**: 22288a, 22304, 26100.   23mm.
38. **1600**: 22288a, 22304; **1601**: 22736(?).   24mm.
39. **1600**: 22288a, 26100.   22mm.
40. **1601**: 6236.   23mm.
41. **1601**: 6236.   22mm.
42. **1601**: 6236; **1606**: 13509(?).   22mm.
43. **1601**: 6237.   24mm.
44. **1601**: 6237.   22, 20, 20mm.
45. **1601**: 6237.   27, 21mm.
46. **1601**: 6237.   24, 23mm.
47. **1601**: 6237; **1603**: 6259.   23, 23, 23mm.
48. **1602**: 5347.   23mm.
49. **1602**: 26026.   21mm.
50. **1603**: 5121; **1604**: 14756; **1607**: 15540(?).   23mm.
51. **1603**: 7084.   23mm.
52. **1603**: 7539.   21mm.
53. **1603**: 13848.   24mm.
54. **1603**: 18041; **1604**: 343.   22mm.
55. **1603**: 18041.   20mm.
56. **1603**: 18041.   22mm.
57. **1603**: 18041.   23mm.
58. **1603**: 18041.   24mm.
59. **1603**: 18041.   28mm.
60. **1603**: 18041.   25mm.
61. **1603**: 18041.   23mm.
62. **1603**: 3068, 13592, 18041; **1604**: 17479; **1605**: 702.1.   22mm.
63. **1603**: 18041.   25mm.
64. **1603**: 18041.   20mm.
65. **1603**: 18041.   21mm.
66. **1603**: 18041.   21mm.
67. **1603**: 18041.   20mm.
68. **1603**: 18041.   21mm.

69. **1603**: 13592; **1605**: 702.1, 21717.   23mm.
70. **1603**: 13592.   19mm.
71. **1603**: 21467.   21, 22, 21mm.
72. **1604**: 343.   20mm.
73. **1604**: 343, 14756.   21mm.
74. **1604**: 343.   19mm.
75. **1604**: 343.   19mm.
76. **1604**: 343, 17481(?), 26040; **1607**: 21461(?).   21mm.
77. **1604**: 2811; **1605**: 7216.   22mm.
78. **1604**: 17429; **1605**: 6071, 6457; **1606**: 5348.   21mm.
79. **1604**: 17429.   24mm.
80. **1604**: 17480.   22mm.
81. **1604**: 22282.   18mm.
82. **1605**: 21717; **1606**: 13509. 21mm.
83. **1605**: 13857.   23mm.
84. **1605**: 6457, 15448.   21mm.
85. **1605**: 15448.   22mm.
86. **1605**: 15448.   22mm.
87. **1605**: 15448; **1606**: 5348.   20mm.
88. **1605**: 15448; **1599**: 26019(?).   21mm.
89. **1605**: 18288, 22766(?); **1607**: 344, 710, 11842, 15535, 15540.   22
mm.
90. **1606**: 4978.   24mm.
91: **1606**: 4978.   24mm.
92. **1606**: 4978.   25mm.
93. **1606**: 5348.   19mm.
94. **1606**: 5348.   21.5mm.
95. **1606**: 5348.   19, 20mm.
96. **1606**: 13509.   23mm.
97. **1606**: 14774.   23mm.
98. **1606**: 14774.   23mm.
99. **1606**: 14774.   21mm.
100. **1606**: 20983.   22.5mm.
101. **1607**: 344.   20mm.
102. **1607**: 344.   25mm.
103. **1607**: 344.   24mm.
104. **1607**: 12255.   20mm.
105. **1607**: 21461.   19mm.
106. **1607**: 23669.   22mm.

107. **1611**: 14646.　24mm.
108. **1611**: 15227.　20, 20mm. The crozier of Basle.[9]

9. I am indebted to Mr. I. A. Shapiro,　Department of English, University of Birmingham, for pointing this out to me.

Chapter V

Some Bibliographical Problems

1. LAYOUT

a. The Title-page: When one reads a Simmes book, one is struck first by the attractiveness of the title-page and the neatness of the book as a whole. The title-pages are always well laid out and never crowded. The typical title-page begins with the title in large letters, then usually some secondary matter in smaller print, an ornament, and the imprint.

One notices that Simmes begins his title-page with large type, and employs smaller founts as he descends the page. Often he devoted the first line of the title-page to the single word "THE." By 1603 he had acquired a block with the single word on it in letters 20mm. high, and used it ten times in the next four years.

The main title of the book is usually in fairly large letters, often a fount with capitals 10mm. high. Sometimes the title is in capitals, sometimes he employed lower case. The lines of type are usually short and uncrowded, and Simmes preferred to split words instead of resorting to longer lines or smaller fount to fit them all in. An example of this is the title-page of the first quarto of *Richard II* (STC 22307) printed in 1597, which begins: "THE | Tragedie of King Ri-| chard the fe-| cond." Here the fount used has 10mm. capitals, and the title stands out clearly in heavy, short lines. In the second edition a year later Simmes cut the title down from four lines to three by having the third line read: "chard t' e fecond."

Simmes did not necessarily retain the same fount when he broke up a word. In the first quarto of *Sir John Oldcastle* (STC 18795), 1600, the two lines "the true and hono-| rable hiftorie . . ." are in different fount sizes, the second line being in letters half the size of the first. Simmes not only changed fount sizes from one line to the other without regard to grammatical units, but also changed type-faces from roman to italic or vice-versa. This can be seen on the title-page of Latimer's *Sermons* (STC 15281) where a word is broken and the type-face changed: "preached by the right Re| *uerend Father*. . ."

It can be seen that the unit Simmes employed was the line of type. If a word had to be broken, the part of the word carried over would be set in the type used for the remainder of the line. While it was usual for each line to be set in a single fount, there were exceptions in cases where the printer wished to emphasize certain words, and here he would introduce capitals or contrasting type as he saw fit. In *Englands mourning garment* (STC 5121), for example, we find the line ". . . for entertainment of King IAMES. . ." The general practice seems to have been that while type-faces and sizes were regularly mixed on the title-page, each line was of a single fount.

There is one peculiarity to be noted here. Simmes rarely used black-letter type on his title-pages. One book, Aesop's *Fables* (STC 182) printed in 1596, has much of its title-page in black-letter, and in two other books printed that year (STC 14802, 23362) there are three lines of black-letter on the title-pages. During the remainder of his career Simmes employed black-letter for two lines of title-page type in 1602 (STC 26026) and one line in 1607 (STC 11842).

On most Simmes title-pages the title of the book is separated from the imprint by a device or ornament. This was almost always done; there are only two books (apart from the tiny thumb-books, STC 25220-2) which have no ornamentation of any kind on the title-page (STC 14802 and 13592). The usual practice was to use a printer's device or a leaf ornament in this place; infrequently did he use a regular ornamental piece.

Simmes made effective use of his flower ornaments, especially numbers 1 and 2. In many cases he made up designs from them and used these to separate title and imprint. In his earlier years Simmes often used the flower for title-page borders. The use of these flower ornaments is one of the characteristic marks of a Simmes book.

The imprint followed a general pattern. "LONDON" or "AT LONDON" was usually set on a line by itself immediately below the ornament, often in small capitals. This was followed by the formula "Printed by Valentine Simmes for . . ."followed by the name of the publisher, and the address of the shop where they were to be sold. It was common practice, especially in the early 1600s, for Simmes to use only his own initials, but the full name of the publisher. We have already noted the practice which Ling imposed upon his printer.

Simmes spelled his name in the usual way, "Simmes," although he occasionally spelled it "Sims." He tried "Sems" once in 1596 (STC 17906) and twice the next year attempted "Symmes" (STC 720, 1828). Only once he altered his first name to "Vallentine" (STC 19180).

The general impression created by the title-pages is that they were carefully laid out with a deliberate attempt to catch the eye. They begin with large type which becomes smaller; the lines tend to shorten as one goes down the page, giving a pyramid effect with the base at the top at the page and the apex at the ornament, followed by the broad base of the imprint. The centering is accurate to a millimetre;

there is no crowding. Simmes realized that to be attractive a title-page had to be simple, so he didn't try to say too much on this important page. The total effect was one of neatness and eye-catching appeal.[1]

b. Head-titles and running-titles: The head-title of a Simmes book commonly repeated what was on the title-page, with little additional information. In some cases where the head-title introduced a section of a book which dealt with several topics, there would be different matter on the head-title. In at least one case Simmes seems to have printed the head-title from standing type used on the title-page (STC 25225). The head-title was usually placed beneath an ornament, and it was very seldom that the head-title was omitted.

Running-title evidence in Simmes's books shows that he generally used one pair of skeletons for his books, and sometimes a single skeleton. This practice would be consistent with the view that Simmes's was a rather small establishment, and that he owned only one press. An example of single-forme setting is *The Pattern of Painful Adventures* (STC 709) a quarto which he printed probably in 1594. A single forme, characterized by a lower case 'p' in 'patterne' is found in the running-titles on sigs. 3v and 4v of each forme until sheet K. At this point a second skeleton was constructed and used in conjunction with the first. The new skeleton (characterized by a broken swash 'e' at the end of 'patterne') was used for inner K and outer L.

Another example of single-skeleton printing, and again early in Simmes's career, was Sir Thomas Smith's *Common-wealth of England* (STC 22860). The running-titles are distinguished primarily by the length of the hyphen in 'Common-wealth', and by a break in the 'E' of 'England'. The single skeleton was used throughout, and only once was it turned so that the variant 'E' appeared on sigs. 1 and 4 instead of 1 and 2.

Simmes commonly used a pair of skeletons, one for the outer forme and one for the inner. The 1603 *Hamlet* illustrates this practice. There is a different pattern of skeletons in *The Shoemakers' Holiday* of 1600. Bowers noted that a pair of skeletons was used, but that one skeleton was used for the inner *and* outer formes of alternate sheets. This was not an isolated case, as other Simmes books show. For example, John Weever's *Faunus and Melliflora* (STC 25225) printed in the same year was printed in this way, with a skeleton characterized by a swash 'M' combined with a defective 'f' was used to set the inner and outer formes of sheets C, E, G, and I.

1. Oliver Simon had a word for them: "Conical." See his "The Title-page" in *The Fleuron* No. 1 (1923), pp.93-7.

It is not unusual to find a mixture of running-title patterns in Simmes's work. For example, in Dedekind's *The Schoole of Slovenrie* (STC 6457) which Simmes printed in 1605, we find a pair of skeletons, one for the outer forme, one for the inner, used in regular progression through sheets B, C, D. In sheet E we find the inner skeleton used for both formes, and then back again to the pair for sheets F to L (with one reversal on sheets I and K). At sheet M there is a new setting, with the single skeleton used for both formes, and then for the rest of the book a pair is used, the new skeleton replacing the one used for the outer formes of the previous sheets.

c. Signatures: The signatures in Simmes's books are regular. A quarto was signed on the recto of the first three leaves of each sheet, and an octavo was signed on the first four leaves. The signature itself consisted of a capital in the same fount as the text, a narrow quad, an arabic number, and no stop. It was positioned somewhat to the right of centre on the same line as the catchword.

The regularity of the order in which the sheets were signed is a feature of Simmes's work. Usually the title-page is on the first page of the first sheet, at A1. A1v is blank, and the preliminaries or text followed on A2. Then the alphabet was regularly followed, with extra leaves or irregularly signed sheets appearing only a very few times. There were some cases in which A1 was blank, with the title-page being A2, but this was not regular practice. Preliminaries, wherever possible, were fitted into the first sheet, with the text beginning on B1. In such cases the first sheet may have been printed last. Occasionally the placing of an errata or contents list in the first gathering indicates that the first sheet was the last printed.

Half sheets were avoided where possible, but they did occur from from time to time. In some such cases both the first and last sheets were halves, and may have been printed together.

d. Pagination: More often than not Simmes books were paginated. The workmanship in the early years was bad, and the pagination of books printed before 1598 is often confused. The errors made by the workmen were usually simple, such as leaving the page numbers in the formes as they printed successive sheets, or simply skipping a few page numbers. As time progressed, however, these errors decreased; at no time were they taken seriously enough to correct as the sheets were being imposed.

Foliation was uncommon in Simmes books. It is interesting to note that Simmes never paginated a dramatic quarto.

2.   PRINTERS' MEASURES*

R. B. McKerrow stated that many composing sticks of different fixed lengths were used in early printing shops.[1] Referring to Blades' study of Caxton, he pointed out that there were at least fourteen different lengths of measure used in Caxton's shop.

In Simmes's printing shop there was a much greater variation in line-lengths, and, if McKerrow was correct, Simmes used no fewer than 42 composing sticks. It would seem much more likely that Simmes's compositors used composing sticks which could be varied in length as required.

An examination of Simmes's books shows that his octavos varied in line-length from 51 mm. to 76 mm., his quartos from 77 mm. to 107 mm., his four folios used lengths of 98, 101, 114, and 130 mm., and his 32mos employed lengths of 22 mm. and 38 mm. There was no favoured length of line in octavos, although six were set at 64 mm.; a length of from 85 to 90 mm. was preferred in quartos. The following table shows the number of books set at the various line-lengths. The first figure is the number of books printed with a particular line-length, and the second figure is the length of the line in millimeters. For example, the first numbers, 1/51, indicate that one book was composed with a line-length of 51 mm.

Octavo format:	1/51	1/59	1/65
	1/52	3/60	2/69
	3/54	1/61	1/70
	1/57	1/63	1/75
	1/58	6/64	1/76
quarto format:	1/77	6/85	4/92
	1/79	2/86	2/93
	3/80	8/87	2/94
	7/81	10/88	2/95
	4/82	18/89	1/98
	5/83	4/90	1/105
	7/84	1/91	1/107

McKerrow noted that certain of Caxton's line-lengths appeared in several books printed in a relatively short space of time, thus suggesting that composing sticks of a fixed length were used until discarded. By contrast, Simmes's most common line-lengths appeared throughout his printing career (1594-1607), as the following tabulation of the seven most common line-lengths shows. This distribution further suggests

*Reprinted with permission from *Studies in Bibliography* XV (1962).

1. *Introduction to Bibliography for Literary Students* (1959), p. 64.

that a stick of variable length was used, and that Simmes selected particular lengths whenever they were called for by the job at hand. The first figure in the tabulation is the number of books printed with a particular line-length, and the second figure is the year in which these books appeared.

64 mm.: 1/1595, 1/1600, 2/1602, 3/1603
81 mm.: 1/1601, 1/1604, 1/1605, 3/1607
84 mm.: 2/1596, 1/1599, 1/1602, 2/1604
85 mm.: 1/1595, 1/1597 1/1599, 1/1603, 1/1604, 1/1605
87 mm.: 4/1596, 2/1597, 1/1598, 1/1599
88 mm.: 1/1595, 1/1598, 2/1600, 2/1601, 2/1602, 1/1603, 1/1607
89 mm.: 1/1597, 1/1599, 6/1600, 1/1603, 3/1604, 1/1605, 3/1606, 2/1607

3. PROOF CORRECTIONS

We are fortunate in having extant an example of Simmes's proof correcting. The outer forme of sheet B in the Bridgewater copy of *1 Contention* (*1600*: STC 26100) contains twenty-one corrections in ink, and the Kemble-Devonshire copy and the two Malone copies have the corrections incorporated into them. This was discovered by Tucker Brooke, who examined the Bridgewater and Kemble-Devonshire copies at the Huntington Library.[1]

Tucker Brooke points out that the compositor followed his corrections carefully, missing only one of the twenty-one changes. He points out further that Simmes seemed to be careful of minor details, as most of the changes are improvements in punctuation or spelling. He suggests that the proof-sheet was not collated with the copy-text, the first quarto of 1594, as a few misprints introduced into the text have been allowed to stand.

There is one important feature which Tucker Brooke did not bring out, however. Sixteen of the twenty-one 'errors' which the proof-reader corrected were made because the compositor had faithfully followed his copy. Sixteen of the errors are actually 'improvements' to the text introduced by the proof-reader, and these are nearly all improvements in punctuation. The proof-reader was, to some extent, an editor.

1. "Elizabethan Proof Corrections in a Copy of *The First Part of the Contention* 1600." *The Huntington Library Bulletin*, No. 2, Nov. 1931, p.87ff.

Listed below are the readings in the copy-text, then the readings in the Bridgewater copy, with the proof corrections in square brackets.

	Q1 copy-text	Bridgewater, Q2
B1r	What angry with your *Nell*,	what[,]angry with your Nell,[-]
B2v	Villaines get you gone	Villaines[,]get ye gone[,]
	againſt me thus.	againſt me thus.[?]
	moue his cap nor ſpeake	moue his cap[,]nor ſpeake
	ſhe vanted	ſhe vaunta[e]d
B3r	with him,	*with him,* [:]
	France, or *York*,	Fraunce[,]or,[-]Yorke,
	himſelfe	himſ[ſ]elfe
	who is King but thee. The	who is King out but thee,[?]the
	Doth as we ſee,	Doth[(]as we ſee,[)]
B4v	vnckle *Gloſter*,	vnckle[ ]Gloſter, [space needed]
	Wherein is	Wherein [i]s
	And here the ſpirit	And he[a]re the ſpirit
	Then *Roger Bullinbrooke*	Then *Roger Bullinbrooke* [,]about
	about	

When copies of Simmes books are collated, variations are seldom found, and the texts are reasonably correct. This could indicate either that Simmes's compositors were careful in their work, or that corrections were made at an early stage of imposition, so that few uncorrected sheets went on the market. Another possibility is that there was a combination of these factors, but the fact remains that Simmes's books show few errors, and little evidence of correction during actual printing.

4.   ERRATA LISTS

Simmes included errata lists in eleven of his books. An examination of the lists reveals nothing of any real interest; Simmes's compositors made the usual kinds of mistakes found in books of this period. There were several cases of apparent misreading of the MS copy-text, as 'Tantens' for 'Tauteus' and 'as' for 'us' (STC 1829), 'clarius' for 'clauius' (STC 26019), 'fellow' for 'follow,' 'with' for 'witte,' 'punike' for 'panike' 'rigor' for 'vigor,' and 'our' for 'one' (STC 18041).

In other cases the errors were caused by the compositor's thinking he knew the words, and then being tricked by faulty memory into substituting similar words for the correct ones. Examples culled from the errata lists are: 'little' for 'like,' 'River' for 'Region,' 'greene' for 'greate,' 'maces' for 'markes,' 'partiall' for 'particular,' 'poſſeſsion' for 'profeſſion,' (STC 94), 'nullique' for 'nulla,' 'whole' for 'holy,' 'ſcarcitie' for 'ſecurity,' and 'ſuccors' for 'ſucceſſe' (STC 11578).

It is of slight interest to note that the compositors sometimes made more important errors by forgetting to insert a negating word. For example, they wrote: 'inhabited' instead of 'not inhabited' (STC 94), 'thou fhalt die' for 'thou fhalt not die' (STC 18041), and 'it was the' in place of 'it was not the' (STC 11578).

5. SHARED PRINTING

Simmes shared the printing of at least sixteen[2] books, and in each case this can be demonstrated bibliographically. In 1596 and '7 Simmes shared the printing of *The Ancient History of the Destruction of Troy* (STC 15379) with Thomas Creede. This book, a quarto in eights, is divided into three parts, each prefaced by a title-page. The first two title-pages, dated 1596, bear Creede's imprint, while the third one, dated 1597, bears Simmes's imprint.

The change in printers took place in the middle of the second part, at the end of the first register, V6v. The book then begins a second register, 2A, instead of completing the alphabet. There is an error in pagination at this point, jumping from page 312 on V6v to 321 on 2A1. This gap would have accommodated one more sheet had Creede needed it; he obviously did not, and no material has been skipped, as the catchword is correct.

The typography changes with the second register; the running-titles are in a smaller type, the type-face itself takes on a lighter appearance, although it is the same size. Then too the size of the type-page changes, becoming smaller. Simmes's ornaments and initials begin to appear almost immediately at 2A2.

There are a few leaves in this book which appear to have been set by a third printer. These leaves are not integral parts of the text, but include a contents list. They are printed on coarse, porous paper and have a black appearance.

In 1599 there were two occasions when second printers were involved with Simmes in printing books. *Nashes Lenten stuff* (STC 18370) has a section, sheets B-F, which was not set by Simmes, but, according to STC, by Thomas Judson. These sheets are characterized by full signing and italicized names, both contrary to Simmes's practices which were to sign quartos three times, and to print names in the same type-face as the rest of the text. In addition, ornaments which did not belong to Simmes are introduced.

2. One example of Simmes's shared printing, the first quarto of Shakespeare's *Richard III*, was noted by Isaacs in 1936, and discussed by Greg in his facsimile edition.

The break between F4v and G1 is obvious. Again we have a change in the size of the type-page, and a change in the type-face itself, from a type giving a fairly light impression to one with broader lines which gives a blacker appearance on the page. There is a running-title change, with the spelling '*prayſe*' changing to '*praiſe*' and a catchword error, in which a name is set in italic on F4v, '*Ariſtip*' and changed to Simmes's preferred roman 'Ariſtippus.'

The remainder of the book, sheets A and G-K4L2, is characterized by the regular Simmes signatures, names set in the type-face of the rest of the text, and by the use of recognized Simmes ornaments.

The second book which Simmes shared this year was Wright's *Certain Errors in Navigation* (STC 26019). This book was printed mainly by Simmes, but contained a short section at the end printed by Edward Aggas. This addition contained some more errors in navigation, and was part of the original work, as Simmes included the proper catchword at the end of his stint.

Aggas began with a new register, signing his sheets A-D4. His work is characterized by being paginated, which Simmes's section was not and by different ornaments. The type appears to have been dirty, and the inking is far too heavy, making it an inferior piece of workmanship when compared with Simmes's.

A Fruitful Meditation[3] is a short octavo, signed A-B8C6, which was printed probably in 1603. The first sheet bears recognized Simmes ornaments and initials, and contains preliminaries. The two remaining sheets were not printed by Simmes. The type used was a black-letter measuring 95mm., and Simmes never employed a fount of this size. There is also an initial 'A' which Simmes used nowhere else in his work. It is possible to suggest that Simmes borrowed an initial 'A' having five of his own, and a complete case of type, all to print two sheets. It is much more reasonable on the evidence to suggest that another printer set up these two sheets for him.

In the two years 1604 and '5 Simmes shared the printing of a surprising number of books. In 1604 there were at least six cases of shared printing, together with five cases the next year. The first was the printing of the first quarto of Dekker's *The Honest Whore* (STC 6501). This case has been fully examined by Professor Bowers, who states that Simmes set only the first two sheets.[4] The second case involved the setting of Wright's *The Passions of the Mind* (STC

3. Not in STC. It is closely related to STC 14377; the two were probably printed within a short time of one another. This edition was found in the Cambridge University Library, shelf mark Syn 8.61.166

4. *The Dramatic Works of Thomas Dekker* (1955) Vol. 3, p. 4.

26040), which has a section in the middle of it, sheets G to O, which was not set by Simmes. There are several points marking off this section. The running-title spelling of the word '*Minde*' changes to '*Mind*' throughout, larger numerals are used for pagination, and the signature numbers are in roman numerals instead of Simmes's undeviating practice of arabic. There is a change in the number of lines per page, dropping from 32 to 31, and initials and factotums not in Simmes's stock are introduced. The use of the factotums is more important, for Simmes never used any but his three regular pieces. Finally, to set off this section, there is a pagination error between O8v and P1.

Simmes joined with George Eld, then at the threshold of his career, in the printing of an edition of *The supplication of certain Mass-priests* (STC 14431) for Aspley. The work can be divided between sheets E and F, with Simmes' type found in the second half of the book.

An important printing venture (at least from our point of view) which Simmes appears to have shared is the printing of the three quartos of Marston's *Malcontent* (STC 17479-81), printed in 1604.[3] A section of each play is characterized by a type which Simmes is not known to have used, a roman 82 with a centre-dot 'i' and a narrow 'k'. In the first quarto sheets B-E have this type, in the second quarto, sheets B-E and the half-sheet I, and in the third quarto, only sheets H and I.

In 1605 there were five more clear cases of shared printing. One of these was again with George Eld, *Remains of a greater work* (STC 4521), which according to the imprint was printed by Eld alone for Simon Waterson. However, only the first sheet, containing preliminaries, and the sheets at the end, on a separate register, containing some added poems, were printed by Eld; the remaining bulk of the book was printed by Simmes.

Another printer who shared his work with Simmes a second time was Thomas Creede. Together they printed Henry Crosse's *The school of policy* (STC 6071), with Creede having the lion's share of the printing, and Simmes doing only the first sheet. This time it was Simmes' name which appeared alone on the imprint as the printer, and the publisher was named as Nathaniel Butter.[4]

---

3. The relationships of these quartos is more fully discussed below p. 94-101.

4. The ornament on B1 is Creede's, although it is similar to Simmes' #10. The ornamental 'T' found in this book has been noted in other Creede books. See Gladys Jenkins: "The Archpriest Controversy and the Printers, 1601-1603," *The Library*, V, Vol. 2 (1947) p. 180.

A more equal division of labour is found in Simmes's edition of Le Loyer's *A treatise of spectres or strange sights* (STC 15448), of which Simmes printed the preliminary sheet and the second half of the book, beginning at sheet L. The printer of sheets B-K, I have not been able to identify, but it may have been Thomas Purfoot. Type matching that of the *Treatise* (type characterized by a narrow 'k' combined with a distinctive but ill-fitting 'w') is found in sheet G of Purfoot's 1606 editions of Marston's *The Fawn* (STC 17483 and 4). Another printer who appeared to have type with similar characteristics was John Windet, and a similar 'k' and 'w' are found scattered throughout his 1606 edition of Marston's *Sophonsiba* (STC 17488).

Lastly, two books of contemporary interest involved Simmes. The highwayman, Gamaliel Ratsey, was hanged on March 6, 1605, and a 'life and death' of Ratsey was entered in the Register to John Trundle on May 2.[5] The title-page is missing from the surviving copy (STC 21753) of the subsequently published book, but it is evident from type and ornaments that Simmes printed the first two sheets. A few weeks later a second part was entered[6] and, according to the title-page, printed by Simmes to be sold by Hodgets under the title of *Ratsey's Ghost* (STC 20753). Again haste was necessary to catch public interest, and Simmes shared the printing. It looks as though, in fact, no fewer than four printers were at work, with Simmes doing sheets A and B, a second printer sheets C and D, a third sheet E, and a fourth sheet F.

6.   THE THIRD PREFACE TO *Mœoniæ*

Simmes printed two editions of Robert Southwell's *Mœoniæ* (STC 22954, 5) in 1595, and the same year James Roberts printed his *St. Peter's Complaint* (STC 22956). Both editions of *Mœoniæ* (the second edition being a page-for-page reprint of the first) contained a dedicatory epistle, "The Printer to the Gentlemen Readers" signed I[ohn] B[usby], on A2 and A2v. The British Museum copy of *St. Peter's Complaint* has, on A2, a dedicatory epistle headed "The Author to his louing Cosin." But, on A2 of the Huntington copy of *St. Peter's Compaint* we find John Busby's epistle from *Mœoniæ*.

This insertion in the Huntington copy is probably a cancel, but as the copy is inlaid it is difficult to be certain. Were the cancel simply a leaf from either extant edition of *Mœoniæ*, it could be understood, as the two books deal with the same series of Southwell poems. It happens that the cancel in the Huntington copy is a third setting of Busby's preface, closely following the other editions, employing the same factotum, and undoubtedly set by Simmes from the preface in

5. Arber III, p. 287.   6. Arber III, p. 291.

one or the other of the extant editions: the variants do not demonstrate from which.

It is highly unlikely that Simmes would print a preface which Roberts would use to cancel some of his own prefaces. The alternative is that Simmes actually printed a third edition of *Mœoniæ* which has not survived, and that, by chance, a copy of its preface has found its way into a copy of *St. Peter's Complaint*. The situation is similar to that of Drayton's *Matilda*, discussed below.

7.   THE THIRD QUARTO OF *Hamlet*

Greg asserts that Simmes printed the third quarto of *Hamlet* in 1611.[5] He makes the claim on the basis of one ornament, number 26 in this study, which Simmes had used once seven years previously. By 1611, however, Simmes's old ornament stock had been taken over by other printers or had disappeared, so the presence of this ornament at this date cannot be taken as evidence that Simmes printed the book.

There are several features of this quarto which point away from Simmes rather than toward him. On the title-page a fount of type is used which is not found in any of Simmes's books. This is the fount of small capitals employed to print "BY WILLIAM SHAKESPEARE." The letters are square in appearance, unlike any fount Simmes used.

Certain typographical features are found in *Hamlet* Q3 which are not found in recognized Simmes books. The signatures on sheets D-G, L all have periods between the letters and the numbers, a practice which Simmes never adopted. Simmes's dramatic texts are noted for the regularly of the treatment of stage-directions and exits, and for the rarity with which we find a mixture of roman and italic type-faces in a text. In the third quarto of *Hamlet* we find that stage-directions and exits are not uniformly treated, and that italic type is introduced into the roman type of the text and, what is even more interesting, roman type introduced into italic stage-directions, a practice Simmes invariably avoided.

The speech-prefixes are, with three exceptions, stopped. This is not too important, as it was only one of Simmes's compositors who habitually left the prefixes unstopped. The prefixes are almost always abbreviated in *Hamlet* Q3, contrary to a common Simmes practice of using unabbreviated tags.

8.   AUTHORS AND DEDICATEES

There are only a few books which tell us anything about Simmes's relations with his authors or patrons. Two books contain dedications

5. *Bibliography*, Vol. 1, p. 311.

signed by Simmes, one being the dedication to *The Poesie of Floured Prayers* (STC 5653) printed in 1611; a formal yet fervent dedication to the Princess Elizabeth. It says nothing revealing, yet is pathetic when one considers Simmes's probable circumstances at the time:

I may not doubt (most gracious lady) but certainly believe, that as you are religiously devoted; so you are sufficiently stored with Meditations, Prayers, and Supplications of Saints, best befitting your Royal Estate: So that by reprinting of these ancient Prayers, and causing them to be disposed to your Graces Name, I may seem to offer a well-known, Princely, and gracious acceptance of all that which proceedeth from well-meaning minds, I have adventured in all humility to offer them unto your most Royal Service, to be respected, or rejected at your pleasure; for whose most happy continuance in this world, and participation of perfect joy in the world to come, I also will not cease to pray to almighty God.

Your Graces most humbly,
Valentine Sims.[6]

The second dedication is an earlier one, in *The Triall of true Friendship* (STC 1053) by M.B., printed in 1596. The dedication is addressed to Walter Flude, Gentlemen. Simmes in his dedication, after confessing "how much charged I stand unto your bountie," goes on to say that he is completely at Flude's service; but apparently this is not a slavish subservience, since the wording points to a real bond of friendship between the two men. The dedication is as follows:

To recognize (sir) in multitude of wordes how much charged I stand unto your bountie, were to your wisedome, I know, but frivolous, who better respecteth the inward service intended of any one (whereof I humbly beseech you on my part to stand assured) than an outward behavior, the validitie whereof manie wayes may be doubted. Yet nevertheless, in that the thoughts of men are onlie in word or action to be desciphered, let it, I beseech you, stand with your good favour, that I may by this little mite of my friendes labours confesse myself bound unto you: and for the residue, when it shal seeme good unto you to commaund mee, I will not have life or abilitie that shall not bee yours, in all it may please you to use me. Thus much to have delivered, may, for the present, satisfie my mind but thus much to have perfourmed, would content my soule, for that in al actions of the body inwardly to be affected, the minde is pleased with speach, and the heart only is replenished by the dooing. Much more to have protested, were no more than sufficient, though more than wherewith your modestie will be pleased, for which, I remaine in heart more than in abilitie to

6. Spelling modernized.

answere the same: humbly submitting my poor service to the censure
thereof, and recommending you unto the protection of the Almightie, and
to the happy possessing of your hearts best content.

> Yours ever affectionate,
> Valentine Simmes.

This same book gives us our only example of a relationship between
Simmes and an author. In the dedication to Flude, Simmes speaks of
the book as "this litle mite of my friendes labours." The author is
known only by his initials, M.B. It is the only book assigned to him in
STC, and a search of STC fails to suggest a known author who could
be identified with it.

There are two instances where Simmes admitted that he had printed
without the author's knowledge. In 1597 a manuscript copy of *Laura.
The toyes of a traueller* (STC 24097) came into his hands through the
agency of a friend. In his preface, Simmes tells how his friend acquired
the manuscript "by mere fortune," and how he himself found it in his
friend's possession "by as great a chaunce." Simmes and his friend
decided to publish the poems, keeping secret the identity of the author;
however, his initials, R.T., appeared on the title-page, either by accident or design. Simmes addressed his preface to "the gentle, and
Gentlemen Readers whatsoever:"

Gentlemen; as the Fencer first maketh a flourish with his weapon, before
he commeth to stroakes, in playing his prize; So I thought good (*pro forma*
onely) to use these few lines unto you before you come to the pith of the
matter. What the Gentleman was that wrote these Verses, I know not; and
what she is for whome they are devised, I cannot ghesse: but thus much I
can say, that as they came into the hands of a friend of mine by mere
fortune; so happned I upon them by as great a chaunce. Onely in this I
must confesse we are both too blame, that whereas he having promised to
keep private the originall, and I the copie, secret: we both have consented
to send it abroad, as common: presuming chiefly upon your accustomed
curtesies; assuring our selves if we may have your protections, wee shall
thinke our selves as safe as *Ulysses* did, when hee was shadowed under the
shield of *Pallas* against furious *Ajax*; so we by your countenances, shal be
sufficiently furnished to encounter against any foule-mouthed Jackes whatsoever. To censure this worke, is for better wittes than mine owne; and it is
for Poets, not for Printers, to give judgment of this matter; yet if I may
be bolde to reporte what I have heard other Gentlemen affirme; many have
written worse, some better, few so well: the worke being so ful of choice &
change, as it thoght it will rather delight every way, than dislike any way.
Thus curteous Gentlemen, building upon my woonted foundation of your

friendly acceptance, I rest your debtors, and will studie in what I can daily to make you amends.

Yours alwayes.

On the last recto page of this book appears "A Frends just excuse about the Booke and Author, in his absence," signed R.B.[7] This friend tells us that the author had heard of the publishing venture and wished to stop it. The author, identified by STC as Robert Tofte, approached R.B., who agreed to stop the edition. However, either by accident or design R.B. did not arrive at the printing shop until the book was almost completed.

R.B.'s attitude seems to have been that Tofte's book should be published, but that he was sorry some poems by another author had been mixed with Tofte's. Nothing could be done about it, and he contented himself with reading the completed sheets and adding the errata on the last page. His "just excuse" was:

Without the Authors knowledge as is before said by the Printer, this Poeme is made thus publiquely knowen; which (with my best indevour) the Gentleman himselfe (suspecting what now prooved too true) at my coming up, earnestly intreated me to prevent. But I came at the last sheetes printing, and finde more than thirtie Sonnets not his, intermixt with his: helpt it cannot be but by the wel judging Reader, who will with lesse paine distinguish betweene them, than I on this sodaine possibly can. To him then I referre that labour, and for the Printers faults past in some of the Bookes, I have gathered them in the next page. With the Author beare I pray ye whom I must intreat to beare with mee.

R. B.

Mr Percy Simpson has discussed this example[8] and believes that Tofte was involved in the printing some time before the sheets were completed. He says this on the basis of the dedication to Lady Lucy Percy, signed by R.T., Tofte offers her the poems, "hoping your Ladiship wil keep them as privately, as I send them unto you most willingly." Simpson comments, "Evidently the author was accessory after the fact, and he must have instructed R.B. to print the dedication to Lady Lucy Percy, while hoping not to lose caste if he kept discreetly in the background."

7. University Microfilms, in supplying a film of this book from the Huntington Library, identify R.B. as Richard Barnfield.

8. Simpson, *Elizabthan Drama.* (1955), pp.184,5.

This view may not be correct. It seems unlikely that an author would ask a dedicatee to keep a book privately, whereas it is a reasonable request with a manuscript. The dedication could well have been in the manuscript copy which came into Simmes's hands, and simply have been printed along with the poems. This explanation would remove Tofte from the publication venture. A more important piece of evidence which makes it appear that Tofte could not have been involved while printing was in progress as Mr. Simpson suggests, is that the dedication appears on page A2 of the octavo volume, with the text beginning on A6:   the regularity of printing points to sheet A's having been printed first, with the other sheets following in alphabetical order.

The second book, a translation by W. Burton of Erasmus's *Seven Dialogues* (STC 10457), was printed in 1606 either without Burton's knowledge and permission, or without his knowledge that it was being printed at that particular time. Either construction can be placed on Simmes's account of the publication: the author "being both absent and unacquainted with the sudden publication of his book." Burton may not have given any permission, but the use of the term "sudden publication" suggests that publication had been arranged but that it was not expected that it would be undertaken for some time.

The last instance of a relationship between Simmes and an author is the general note appended to *The Song of Songs* (STC 2771) by the translator, Henoch Clapham. After listing his published works, Clapham addressed a plea "To all Printers:"   "If any of you shall attempt to re-print any of the former Bookes of mine, I pray you (if it may be) let mee first have notice thereof: that so I may better the same in something." The remark does not tell us much about Simmes, but it does add to our growing conviction that authors had small right to their books after publication.

9.   *The Malcontent* QUARTOS, 1604

John Marston's play, *The Malcontent*, was entered in the Stationers' Register on July 5, 1604 to Thomas Thorpe and William Aspley, and the same year Simmes printed three separate editions for Aspley. The quartos differ in length and content, and the main problem is the establishment of the order of their printing.

Sir Walter Greg suggested an order in 1921[1] and this order has come to be generally accepted. A study more detailed than that attempted in 1921 bears out Greg's order. The quartos are entered in

1. *The Library*, Series 4, Vol. 2, 1921, pp. 49-57.

STC as 17479, 17480, and 17481, and will be referred to as Q1, 2, and 3 respectively.

Q1 and Q2 are closely related, as one is a page-for-page reprint of the other, with allowance made for some additional material. Standing type was used in printing the inner forme of sheet D, the outer and inner formes of sheet E, and a single page of outer D, D4v. Sheet A is partly identical, with A3v and 4, and part of A3 having been printed from standing type. All such sheets were, however, revised to some extent. It may be noted in passing that the running-titles of sheets B-E are identical in both editions.

Q2 and Q3 are related, but more in common readings than in common type. Only the title-pages of these editions may be related typographically, as there is the possibility that the imprint was left standing. There are over 25 instances where the reading of Q2 differs from that of Q1, and in which Q3 has followed the Q2 reading. In most cases the Q2-3 readings are corrections of the Q1, although there are a few cases where the reading has been corrupted. Q3 is much longer than either Q1 or 2, as it incorporates an induction and several additional scenes. No attempt was made to reprint page-for-page.

The order of the printing of the quartos can be more firmly established than Greg suggested. It must be admitted, though, that this is not an easy task, as Simmes was a careful workman, and not too many of the differences in the editions are of real consequences. There are, for example, differences such as the reading in Q1 of the word 'raue' which in Q2 and 3 reads 'rand'. In the context either word is correct, and either could have been the original in the manuscript copy. In determining which edition came first, it is necessary to find errors which could not have come from the printed copy, but can be explained only as misreadings of the manuscript. There are several examples which point to Q1 as having manuscript and not printed copy for its source.

On B3v of Q1 appears the reading "the danghrer of the Florentine," corrected in Q2 to "the daughter of the Florentine." This appears to be a case where the compositor of Q1 must have been working from manuscript copy. Were he working from Q2 at this point, one would have to posit that in one word he both turned a letter and made a foul case error (a bad one too, as 'r' and 't' were not close to each other in the case). If the compositor were working from manuscript copy, it is straightforward to argue that he came upon an illegible word, and tried his best to follow his copy.

A similar mistake occurred on H2v of Q1, where Beancha asks the question, "is he not a pretty dapper windle gallant?" to which Maquerelle answers, "He is even one of the most busy fingerd lords." Q2 changes the word 'windle' to 'unidle,' a reading which the text obviously calls for. Again, it seems an odd error to make if the compositor were working from printed copy — if Q1 were printed from Q2, but if Q1 were printed from MS copy, then it is quite obviously a minim error, misreading 'uni' for the very similar 'wi'.

There are other errors which seem to come from MS and not from printed copy. On H3 Q1 prints the end of Maria's speech and Aurelia's entrance:

> Die like a Bride, poore heart thou shalt die chaste.
> *Enter* Aurelia *in mourning habit.*
> *Life is a frost of could felicitie,*
> *Aur. And death the thaw of all our vanitie.*

Q2 corrects this by moving the prefix up one line, giving the whole speech to Aurelia. This is obviously correct, as the speech, set off in italics, is a proverbial couplet. In manuscript such an error could be easily made if the prefixes were in the margin, and not quite opposite the right lines, but it is difficult to understand a careful compositor making the error from printed copy.

The last speech of Q1 was badly handled. Malevole is directing his remarks to the various people around him, and in the margin are the names of the persons to whom he is speaking. It is difficult to determine from the marginal stage directions what remarks are meant for whom. This is further complicated by the fact that one of the stage directions gets into the text itself:

> You to your vowes, to *Pietro & Aurelia,* and thou vnto the
> (subeurbs.

Q2 does not suffer from this confusion, but removes the direction to the margin.

Another direction, "Malevole kicks out Mendozo," was misplaced in the first quarto, being centred and placed before the line on which the action rested. Q2 has throughout this speech made proper sense of the marginal directions, and is obviously correct. Again, it is difficult to see how a compositor could have made such nonsense out of printed copy, but it is quite easy to posit that manuscript copy, with the directions written in at the appropriate line could have been before the compositor as he set Q1.

Sir Walter Greg in 1921 noted that on B2 Q1 omitted a line supplied in Q2: "I am wearie, would I were one of the Duke's hounds now." Both Q1 and Q2 reply with the line: "But what's the common newes abroade *Malevole*, thou dogst rumor still." As Greg points out, these last words are a pun on the reference to hounds, and the line must have stood in the original manuscript copy, and been omitted by the compositor of Q1.

While the reliance of Q2 on Q1 is quite evident, that of Q3 is not so clear. Many of the points of similarity can be explained as the use of the same manuscript (Q2 corrected from manuscript, and Q3 printed directly from it, with additions).

There are, however, a few instances where Q3 has copied the peculiarities of Q2, peculiarities which would not have derived from a manuscript. Perhaps the most important of these is the treatment of the stage direction and scene division at IV,2. All quartos agree here in giving first the stage direction, and then SCENA SECVUNDA follows, contrary to usual usage. It is unlikely that this error derives from manuscript and that each succeeding quarto simply followed its predecessor.

An interesting line on F3 of Q2:

> *Omnes, Mendoza*:   Cornets florish.

has been taken by Q3 to read:

> *Omnes Mendoza.*   Cornets florish.

Here the Q3 compositor has made two errors. He did not realize that *Omnes*, with the unusual comma was, in fact, a speech prefix. Therefore he moved it to the inner margin and removed the comma. More significantly, the Q2 compositor had set the stage direction, 'Cornets florish' in roman instead of italic, and Q3 followed his copy and set the same fount.

The treatment of the last speech in the play also indicates that Q3 was copied from Q2. The second quarto tidied up the marginal stage directions, and used both a star and section mark to indicate which lines were addressed to which characters. These markings were followed by Q3, which also followed Q2's arrangement of the marginal directions.

Several times Q3 has followed the spacing of Q2, a matter which is seldom copied from manuscript copy. For example, on H1v Q2 prints the line:

> *Murder, fame and wrong. Enter Celso.*   Celzo?

Q3, printing the same passage on H4v, has removed the stage direction, which is a repeated direction and should be excised, but he has followed Q2 in setting the word 'Celzo' to the right, apart from the remainder of the speech. It can be noted in passing that he also followed the unusual spelling of the name.

Two other examples of unusual spacing occur in this text. On G1 Q3 follows the spacing of the words '*scelus*. How' found in his Q2 copy in F3v. This is similar to the above example, where the speaker is turning his attention to new matter. Again, on the next page Q3 follows his copy in setting 'Go to then, thou', both quartos spacing the comma a quad away from its proper position.

An important example of Q3 following the spacing of Q2 is found in the following speech by Malevole, who complains to Mendoza:

> *Mal.* Your diuelships ring haz no vertue, the buffe-cap-
> taine, the sallo-westfalian gamon-faced zaza, cries
> stand out, must have a stiffer warrant . . . (F4)

After the word 'cries' there is ample room for the Q2 compositor to print the word 'stand', but, wanting to set off the quote presumably, he does not do so. The Q3 compositor (on G1v) decided to do the same, and he too left the line of type at 'cries', filling in with quads. He, however, came to this point with almost 30mm. to spare, and so left a noticeable gap.

The placing of two speeches on one line is sometimes resorted to by a compositor either if he wishes to justify a page, or if he is carefully copying. There are cases where Q3 has followed the lead of the Q2 copy and placed two short speeches on the same line. When we find instances of following a previous quarto in such double setting it would be assumed that the second was set from a copy of the first. (Instances occur on F3-G1, H3-I1v, H3-I2, H3v-I2.)

There are two examples of progressive correction through the three editions which make any order of printing other than the one suggested incomprehensible. Q1 began by making a blunder in placing half a line in the speech of the next character. The result was that Mendozo finished his speech on F4:

> Skud quicke.
> *Pietro   Like lightning good deedes crawle, but mischiefe flies.*

The Q2 compositor, thinking apparently that the italicized line was a quotation at the end of Mendozo's speech, removed the speech-prefix which assigned the line to Pietro. Q3 made the logical correction, so that the passage read:

> Skud quicke like lightning.
> *Pie.* "*Good deedes crawle but mischiefe flies.*   (G1v)

It is difficult to imagine that a compositor, working from a copy of Q3, could have made the error as found in Q2. The passage makes excellent sense as it stands. It is, however, logical to suggest that the Q1 compositor had difficult with the lines in his manuscript that Q2 working from a copy of Q1 made some sense out of the line, and that it was finally corrected by the time it reached the third quarto.

There is a second passage which shows progressive correction. Greg noted it, and used it in his argument for assuming the order of Q1 and 2. Q1 in the middle of a verse passage on E1, combines two lines into one:

> Yet still the shaft stick fast, so, A good simile my honest
> (Lord,

This is obviously wrong. The person doing proof correction on type left, otherwise, standing, noticed the error, and, having room to spare on this page, moved the line "A good simile my honest Lord" to the next line. He had to assign a speaker to it, and he carelessly assigned Mendozo, who had left the stage three lines before. Q3, however, realized that Q2 was correct in assigning the line to another speaker, caught the error of assigning it to the wrong person, and corrected the prefix to Bilioso. Again, it is difficult to imagine the readings to have occurred in any different order.

The *Malcontent* quartos arc remarkable for their errors in the use of the question mark. In Q1 there are 241 correctly placed question marks, 66 omitted where the sense of the passage requires them, and 23 which are patently wrong. Q2 has added about 20 of the omitted marks, has corrected five of the errors, and added three of its own. Q3 has gone the farthest toward correcting these errors; it has omitted 47 marks where they are required, and corrected all but eleven of the wrong ones. This progressive correction is obvious in some cases, and it would be difficult to suggest any other explanation than that the Q1 compositor made an error in his manuscript copy, and that it was progressively corrected. For example, on H3 Q1 has Mendozo ask, at the unwelcome entrance of Aurelia, "Who? let her in." Q2 follows the error, but Q3 corrects to "Who let her in?"

Another example occurs on E4v, where both Q1 and 2 (in the forme which was not reset) give us the exclamation: "good heauen that fooles should stumble vpon greatnesse?" Q3 reset this with an exclamation mark instead of the question mark. This leads to the suggestion that the manuscript copy from which Q1 was set was characterized by the use of vertical strokes for marks of punctuation, and that the compositor was often fooled by this device, either into reading the mark as a question mark, or into relying upon his own wits and using other punctuation. It is difficult to see how this type of punctuation error could have increased through three editions of a play. Simmes's compositors certainly had their own ideas about dramatic punctuation, but they did not make many flat-out errors. Much more common was the choice of a colon for a comma, or the decision to use a comma where no mark of punctuation existed in the copy. This type of error, however, is foreign to Simmes's workmen, and the logical suggestion is that it stems from copy.

There are several pieces of evidence which corroborate the order suggested for the quartos. Individually they are not conclusive, but their cumulative effect is considerable. An interesting correction, for example, was made from Q1 to Q2 and Q3. The first quarto spelled the villain's name 'Mendozo'. It appeared this way in the *Dramatis personae* of all three editions, and was spelled so 35 of the 41 times the full name appeared in Q1. But, in Q2 it was spelled 'Mendoza,' just as consistently: 34 of the 40 times it was printed in full. Q3 was just as consistent in spelling it with the 'a' ending: 45 of the 51 occurrences. An examination of other Marston plays suggests that this is the way it was usually spelled, and that the 'o' spelling was an error on the part of the compositors. For example, the name Mendoza Fascari appears in *The Insatiate Countess*, and other Italian names ending in 'a' are found in other plays (eg., Gniaca and Claridiana in *The Insatiate Countess*, and Andrea in *What you Will*.) This deliberate changing of the spelling of the name (including changes on the undistributed E4v) is corroborative evidence that Q1 was the first edition of the play.

Another piece of corroborative evidence is the change made on the undistributed A3. Here, one word in Q1 is set in type much larger than that of the remainder of the page; the word, ELEGANTISSIMO, is, of course, an adjective, and, as such, does not deserve any prominence. The Q2 compositor realized this and changed it to the same fount as the remainder of the page. Again, it is difficult to imagine a compositor deliberately making an unnecessary change, while it is quite reasonable to assume that a change to improve the appearance of the page would be made. Q3, of course, follows Q2.

Turning to Q3, there are several features about it which make it reasonable to place it at the end of progression of texts instead of at the beginning. On the *Dramatis personae* page there appears the name 'Pasarello Foole to Bilioso.' This name does not appear in the list of male characters, as one would expect, but at the bottom of the page, after the list of female characters. This in itself is odd. It is made clearer, however, by the realization that Pasarello does not appear in the text as provided by either Q1 or Q2, but is found only in the passages unique to the third quarto. The very positioning of his name suggests that he is an addition to the text, and not an integral part of the play as it first appeared.

Scholars are loath to accept what characters actually say about the text but one remark about the play fits in extremely well. In the induction found in Q3 there is the following exchange between Sly and Burbage:

Sly: What are your additions?

Bur: Sooth not greatly needefull, only as your sallet to your greate feast, to entertaine a little more time, and to abridge the not received custome of musicke in our Theater. . .[2]

This comment fits the additional passages perfectly. For the most part complete in themselves, these scenes introduce a clown, Pasarello, and permit him and his master Bilioso to entertain the audience by making fools of themselves. The result is to heighten the court satire of the play, but to add nothing to either serious characterization or to the plot. In other words, the play could quite conceivably have been written without these scenes being originally contemplated.

---

2. A4. The latter half of Burbage's reply has been glossed by Hazelton Spencer as "Shorten the musical interludes customary at the children's performances but not usual here." *Elizabethan Plays* (Boston, 1933), p. 563. The word sallet, usually understood as meaning salad, could, according to OED, be a jocular reference to a measure of wine.

Bibliography

A. Books

Allison, A.F. and D.M.Rogers: *A Catalogue of Catholic books in English printed abroad or secretly in England, 1558-1640.* Bognor Regis, 1956

Ames, Joseph: *Typographical Antiquities.* London, 1749.

Arber, Edward: *A Transcript of the Registers of the Company of Stationers of London: 1554-1640 A.D.* London, 1950.

Bowers, Fredson: *The Dramatic Works of Thomas Dekker.* Princeton, 1953—.

————: *Principles of Bibliographical Description.* Princeton, 1949.

Greg, Sir Walter W.: *A Bibliography of the English Printed Drama to the Restoration.* London, 1939—.

———— and Boswell, E.: *Records of the Court of the Stationers' Company 1576-1602 —from Register B.* London, 1930.

Jackson, William A.: *Records of the Court of the Stationers' Company 1602 to 1640.* London, 1957.

McKerrow, Ronald B.: *A Dictionary of Printers and Booksellers in England, Scotland and Ireland, and of Foreign Printers of English books, 1557-1640.* London, 1910.

————: *An Introduction to Bibliography for Literary Students.* Oxford, 1928.

————: *Printers' and Publishers' Devices in England & Scotland 1485-1640.* London, 1949.

———— and Ferguson, F. S.: *Title-Page Borders used in England and Scotland 1485-1640.* London, 1932.

Morrison, Paul G.: *Index of Printers, Publishers and Booksellers in A.W. Pollard and G.B. Redgrave A Short-title Catalogue . . .* Charlottesville, 1950 and 1961.

Pierce, W.: *An Historical Introduction to the Marprelate Tracts.* London, 1908.

Pollard, A. W. and Redgrave, G. R.: *A Short-title Catalogue of books printed in England, Scotland & Ireland and of English books printed abroad 1475-1640.* London, 1950.

Simpson, Percy: *Elizabethan Drama,* Oxford, 1955.

Walker, Alice: *Textual Problems in the First Folio.* Cambridge, 1953.

B. Articles

Brooke, C. F. Tucker: "Elizabethan Proof Corrections in a Copy of *The First Part of the Contention* 1600," *The Huntington Library Bulletin.* Los Angeles, 1931.

Heawood, Edward: "Sources of Early English Paper Supply," *The Library.* Oxford, 1930.

Hinman, Charlton: "Shakespeare's Text — Then, Now and Tomorrow," *Shakespeare Survey 18*. Cambridge, 1965.

McKerrow, Ronald B.: "Edward Allde as a typical trade printer," *The Library*. Oxford, 1929.

Meynell, Francis, and Stanley Morison: "Printers' Flowers and Arabesques," *The Fleuron*, No. 1, 1923.

Miller, C. Williams: "A London Ornament Stock: 1598-1683," *Studies in Bibliography, Vol VII*. Charlottesville, 1955.

Simon, Oliver: "The Title-page," *The Fleuron*, No. 1, 1923.

Stevenson, Allan H.: "Watermarks are Twins," *Studies in Bibliography, Vol. IV*. Charlottesville, 1951.

The Books Printed By Valentine Simmes

1594

STC	709	APOLLONIUS OF TYRE. *The patterne of painefull aduentures*
	7206	DRAYTON, MICHAEL. *Matilda*
	20996.2	RICH, BARNABY. *Rich his farewell to Militaire profession*
	22860	SMITH, SIR THOMAS. *The Common-wealth of England*

1595

	3012	BIBLE. *The Kings Psalmes*
	3314	*The gentlemans academie, or the booke of S. Albans*
	4042	BULLEIN, WILLIAM. *The gouernment of health*
	4101	BUNNY, FRANCIS, *A suruey of the popes supremacie*
	4102	BUNNY, FRANCIS. *Truth and falshood*
	7299	DU JON, FRANÇOIS, THE ELDER. *De peccato primo Adami*
	10418	*A myrrour for English souldiers*
	12161	GRAFTON, RICHARD. *A briefe treatise containing many proper tables*
	15638	LINAKER, ROBERT. *A comfortable treatise*
	22954	SOUTHWELL, ROBERT. *Mœoniæ*
	22955	SOUTHWELL, ROBERT. *Mœoniæ* (Another edition)
	22971	SOUTHWELL, ROBERT. *The triumphs over death*
	23361	STRIGELIUS, VICTORINUS. *A third proceeding in the harmonie of King Davids harp*

1596

	182	AESOP. *The fables of Esop in English*
	720	APULEIUS, LUCIUS. *The eleuen bookes of the golden asse*
	1053	B., M. *The triall of true friendship*
	1828	BELL, THOMAS. *The speculation of vsurie*
	1829	BELL, THOMAS. *The suruey of popery*
	13252	HESTER, JOHN. *The first (second) part of the key of philosophie*
	14802	JOSEPH BEN GORION, pseud. *A compendious historie of the Iewes common weale*
	15281	LATIMER, HUGH, Bp. *Fruitfull sermons*

17126.1 M., C. *The first part of the nature of a woman*
19180 PARACELSUS. *A hundred and foureteene experiments and cures*
20797 RECORD, ROBERT. *The castle of knowledge*
22972 SOUTHWELL, ROBERT. *The triumphs over death*
23362 STRIGELIUS, VICTORINUS. *A fourth proceeding in the harmony of King Davids harp*
24249 *A treatise shewing the possibilities of the reall presence*

1597

749 ARIOSTO, LUDOVICO. *Two tales translated out of Ariosto by R. T.*
3942 BRUNO, VINCENZO. *A short treatise on the sacrament of penaunce*
15379 LE FÈVRE, RAOUL. *The auncient historie of the destruction of Troy*
17323 MARGARET, OF ANGOULEME. *The queene of Nararres tales*
17906 MIDDLETON, THOMAS. *The wisdome of Solomon paraphrased*
22307 SHAKESPEARE, WILLIAM. *The tragedie of King Richard the second*
22314 SHAKESPEARE, WILLIAM. *The tragedy of King Richard the third*
24097 TOFTE, ROBERT. *Laura. The toyes of a traueller*

1598

1047 B., J. *A treatise with a Kalendar*
3216 BOIARDO, MATTEO MARIA. *Orlando inamorato. The three first books*
3696 BRETON, NICHOLAS. *A solemne passion of the soules loue*
10253 *Articles to be enquired of within the Dioces of London*
12099 GOSSON, STEPHEN. *The trumpet of warre. A sermon*
16667 LODGE THOMAS. *Rosalynde*
17760 *The meane in spending*
21311 ROMEI, ANNIBALE, Count. *The courtiers academie*
22308 SHAKESPEARE, WILLIAM. *The tragedie of King Richard the second*
22309 SHAKESPEARE, WILLIAM. *The tragedie of King Richard the second* (another ed.)
24477 TYRO, T. *Tyros roring megge*

1599

4987 CHAPMAN, GEORGE. *A pleasant comedy entituled: An humerous dayes myrth*
12273 GREENE, ROBERT. *Menaphon*
17994 MOFFETT, THOMAS. *The silkwormes, and their flies*
18370 NASH, THOMAS. *Nashes Lenten stuffe*
24003 THOMAS, LEWIS. *Seauen sermons*
25089 *A warning for faire women*

25224   WEEVER, JOHN. *Epigrammes in the oldest cut, and newest fashion*

26019   WRIGHT, EDWARD. *Certaine errors in nauigation*

1600

3675   BRETON, NICHOLAS. *Pasquils mad-cap and his message*

3679   BRETON, NICHOLAS. *Pasquils passe, and passeth not*

6523   DEKKER, THOMAS. *The shomakers holiday*

6798   *The lawes and statutes of the stannarie of Deuon*

11578   GARDINER, SAMUEL. *A pearle of price*

17885.1 MIDDLETON, THOMAS. *The ghost of Lucrece*

18795   *The first part of Sir John Oldcastle*

20150   POWEL, GABRIEL. *The resolued Christian, exhorting to resolution*

21466   RUTHVEN, JOHN, THIRD EARL GOWRIE. *The Earle of Gowries conspiracie*

22288   SHAKESPEARE, WILLIAM. *The second part of Henrie the fourth*

22304   SHAKESPEARE, WILLIAM. *Much adoe about nothing*

24152   TOURNEUR, CYRIL. *The transformed metamorphosis*

25225   WEEVER, JOHN. *Faunus and Melliflora*

26100   *The first part of the contention betwixt the two famous houses of Yorke and Lancaster*

1601

6236   DANIEL, SAMUEL. *The works of Samuel Daniel newly augmented*

18893   *Newes from Ostend of the oppugnation*

18894   *Further newes of Ostend*

19343   PARRY, WILLIAM. *A new and large discourse of the trauels of Sir Anthony Sherley*

20053   PLUTARCH. *Inimicus amicus*

20167   POWELL, THOMAS. *The passionate poet*

22736   SMITH, HENRY. *Three sermons*

25226   WEEVER, JOHN. *The mirror of martyrs*

25765   WILMOTT, R. *Syrophaenissa, or the Cananitish womans conflicts*

26039   WRIGHT, THOMAS. *The passions of the minde*

1602

1556   BASSE, WILLIAM. *Three pastoral elegies*

2771   *The Song of Songs . . . expounded . . . by* HENOCH CLAPHAM

5347   CLAPHAM, JOHN. *The historie of England*

6336   DAVIES, JOHN, of Hereford. *Mirum in modum: a glimpse of Gods glorie and the soules shape*

6373   DAVISON, FRANCIS. *A poetical rapsody*

16661   LODGE, THOMAS. *Paradoxes against common opinions*

17621   MASON, ROBERT. *Reasons monarchie*

20151 POWEL, GABRIEL. *The resolued Christian*

24004 THOMAS, LEWIS. *Seauen sermons*

26026 WRIGHT, LEONARD. *A display of dutie*

1603

3068 BILSON, THOMAS, Bp. *A sermon preached at Westminster befor the King and Queenes Maiesties, at their coronations*

5121 CHETTLE, HENRY. *Englands mourning garment . . . in memorie of their sacred mistresse, Elizabeth*

6258 DANIEL, SAMUEL. *A panegyrike congratulatorie to the kings maiestie; also certaine epistles*

6259 DANIEL, SAMUEL. [Another issue, with a new title-page and the addition of the '*Defence of ryme*'.]

7084 DOVE, JOHN. *A perswasion to the English recusants*

7539 EGERTON, STEPHEN. *A lectuur*

13592 HOLLAND, HUGH. *Pancharis: the first booke*

13848 HOTMAN, JEAN. *The ambassador*

14377 JAMES I, King. *A fruitfull meditation*

15355 LEECH, ANDREW. *Iovis arbitrium*

18041 MONTAIGNE, MICHEL DE. *The essayes . . . done into English by . . . Iohn Florio*

20170 POWELL, THOMAS. *A Welch bayte to spare prouender*

21467 RUTHVEN, JOHN, THIRD EARL GOWRIE. *The Earle of Gowries conspiracie*

22275 SHAKESPEARE, WILLIAM. *The tragicall historie of Hamlet Prince of Denmarke*

25221 WEEVER, JOHN. *An Agnus Dei*

1604

94 ACOSTA, JOSEPH DE. *The naturall and morall historie of the East and West Indies*

343 ALEXANDER, WILLIAM, EARL OF STIRLING. *The monarchick tragedies*

2811=3735 *Sacro-sanctum Novum Testamentum*

6501 DEKKER, THOMAS. *The honest whore*

12058 GORDON, JOHN. *England and Scotlands happinesse: in being reduced to vnitie of religion*

14756 JONSON, BENJAMIN. *B. Jon: his part of King James his . . . entertainement*

17429 MARLOWE, CHRISTOPHER. *The tragicall history of D. Faustus*

17479-81 MARSTON, JOHN. *The Malcontent*

20889 RENNECHERUS, HERMAN. *The golden chayne of salvation*

22282 SHAKESPEARE, WILLIAM. *The history of Henrie the fourth*

26040 WRIGHT, THOMAS. *The passions of the minde in generall*

1605

702.1 APHTHONIUS, SOPHISTA. *Aphthonii progymnasmata*

1457 BARLOW, WILLIAM, Bp. of Lincoln. *The summe and substance of the conference*
1597 BAXTER, NATHANIEL. *Praefactio in commentarios*
3058 BIGNON, JEROME. *A briefe but effectual treatise of the election of popes*
6071 CROSSE, HENRY. *The schoole of pollicie*
6457 DEDEKIND, FRIEDRICH. *The schoole of slovenrie*
6502 DEKKER, THOMAS. *The Honest whore*
7216 DRAYTON, MICHAEL. *Poems by Michaell Draiton Esquire*
13857 *The royal entertainement of the . . . Earle of Nottingham*
15448 LE LOYER. PIERRE. *A treatise of specters or straunge sights*
17135 M., H., of the Middle Temple. *The strange fortune of Alerane*
18288 *Two most unnaturall and bloodie murthers*
20753 *The life and death of G. Ratsey*
20753a *Ratseis ghost*
21717 SANDYS, SIR EDWIN. *A relation of the state of religion*
22766 SMITH, HENRY. *Two sermons*

1606

4978 CHAPMAN, GEORGE. *The gentleman usher*
5348 CLAPHAM, JOHN. *The historie of Great Britannie*
10457 ERASMUS, DESIDERIUS. *Seven dialogues both pithie and profitable*
13509 HIND, JOHN. *Eliosto libidinoso*
14774 JONSON, BENJAMIN. *Hymenaei*
20983 RICH, BARNABY. *Faultes, faults, and nothing else but faultes*
25222 WEEVER, JOHN. *An agnus Dei*

1607

344 ALEXANDER, WILLIAM, EARL OF STIRLING. *The Alexandrean tragedie*
710 APOLLONIUS, of Tyre. *The patterne of painful adventures*
6785 DES PORTES, PHILIPPE. *Rodomonths infernall*
6930 DOBSON, GEORGE. *Dobsons Drie Bobbes*
11842 GIBSON, THOMAS, Minister. *Meditations vpon the hundred and sixteene Psalme*
12255 GREENE, ROBERT. *Greenes neuer too late*
13317 HEYWOOD, THOMAS. *The fayre mayde of the Exchange*
15535 LEVER, CHRISTOPHER. *A Crucifixe*
15540 ————. *Queene Elizabeths teares*
21461 RUSSELL, WILLIAM. *The reporte of a bloudie and terrible massacre in the citty of Mosco*
23669 *The taming of a shrew*

1611

14646 *The first and second part of the troublesome raigne of John King of England*

15227 LANYER, ÆMILIA. Mrs. *Salve Deus Rex Iudæorum*

1612

17844 *The most famous and renowned historie of that woorthie and illustrous knight Meruine*

Broadsheets

Two broadsheets printed by Simmes are found in the *Collection of Printed Broadsheets in the possession of the Society of Antiquaries of London,* compiled by Robert Lemon in 1866. They are listed by the collection number:

108 *Weepe with Ioy. A lamentation, for the losse of our late Soueraigne Lady Queene Elizabeth, with ioy and exultation for our high and mightie Prince, King Iames, her lineal and lawfull successor* [1603]

119 *In the time of Gods visitation by sicknesse, or mortality especially, may be used by governours of families* [no date]

Lost Books

Two books by Simmes, no longer extant, are listed in Ames' *Typographical Antiquities,* Vol.2, p.1290. Listed according to date, they are:

1596 *God wooing his Church: set foorth in three godly sermons.* By William Burton, preacher at Reading

1600 *Cato Christianus. In quem coniiciuntur ea omnia, quae in sacris literis ad parentum, puerorumque pietatem videntur maxime pertinere*

Lost Broadsheets

1598 *The Table of Good Counsell with a Singular Salve for the Syck Soule*

1603 *The Traitours Lately Arrayned at Winchester*

Simmes Books not consulted

The following are listed in *STC,* often in unique copies. I was unfortunately unable to visit the libraries in which they were held.

1595 22418 *Shepherds' Kalendar*

1596 12162 GRAFTON, RICHARD. *A brief treatise*

17905 MIDDLETON, THOMAS. *The Wisdom of Solomon paraphrased*

1597 10356 Visitation Articles: *Winchester*

1601 25220 WEEVER, JOHN. *An Agnus Dei*

1603 2772 *Song of Songs*

7085 DOVE, JOHN. *A perswasion to the English recusants*

INDEX

Adams, Thomas, 12, 14, 16, 25
Aggas, Edward, 87
Agnus Dei, 20, 23, 24,
Allde, Edward, 12n
Allde, Mistress, 8
Allison, F. and D.M. Rogers, 16n, 17n
Ames, Joseph, 18n, 109
Ancient history . . . of Troy, 17, 86
Arber, E. A., *passim*
Aspley, William, 18-20, 22-3, 25, 88, 94

Bailey, John, 21
Baines, Robert, 7
Ballard, Henry, 9n, 41, 43, 45, 50-4, 61-4
Bancroft, *Bishop*, 7
Barker, Christopher, 53
Barker, Robert, 62
Barley, William, 17, 51
Barnes, John, 20
Barnfield, Richard, 93n
Blades, William, 83
Blagden, Cyprian, 5n, 7n, 10n
Blount, Edward, 21-2, 24-5
Blower, Ralph, 10, 25, 52, 60
Bodley, John, 6, 7n
Bonian, Richard, 25
Boseman, William 9
Boswell, E. See Greg & Boswell
Bowers, Fredson, 22n, 35, 87
Boyle, Richard, 14
Brooke, Tucker, 84
Budge, John, 24
Bunny, Francis, 14
Burre, Walter, 20-2
Burby, Cuthbert, 8n, 18, 21
Busby, John, 12, 14, 16, 19, 25, 89
Bushell, Thomas, 18, 20, 22, 25, 44
Butter, Nathaniel, 23, 25, 88
Bynneman, Henry, 5, 50

Cadman, Thomas, 44
Cato Christianus, 18, 109
Caxton, William, 83
Certain errors in navigation, 87
Chorlton, Geoffrey, 23
Clapham, Henoch, 94
Commonwealth of England, 12, 81
Cooke, Matthew, 24
Cowper, Richard, 6, 7n

Creede, Thomas, 17-9, 25, 40, 60, 64, 86, 88
Crowley, Charles, 8

Derby, *Earl of*, 6
Display of duty, 20
Doctor Faustus, 22, 25
Eld (e) , George, 10, 22, 50n, 88
Eliosto libidinoso, 23, 41
Elizabeth, *Princess*, 91
Englands mourning garment, 80
Epigrams (Weever) , 18
Essays (Montaigne) , 21, 25
Everyman out of his humour, 27n

Fables (Aesop) , 80
Fair maid of the Exchange, 24
Faunus & Melliflora, 81
Fawn, The, 89
Ferbrand, William, 23
Ferguson, F. S., See McKerrow & Ferguson
First part of the Contention, 19, 27-37, 84
Flower, Francis, 7
Flude, Walter, 91-2
Four Sermons (Smith) , 23
Fruitful meditation, 21, 87

Gentlemans academy, 14
Gentleman Usher, 23
God wooing his Church, 109
Gods arrows, 45
Golden Ass, 15
Golden chain of salvation, 22
Government of health, 6, 15
Greg, Sir Walter, 27n, 53, 86n, 90, 94-7
Greg, Sir Walter and E. Boswell, 5n, 7n, 8n
Griffen, Edward, 10

Hall, Rowland, 43, 45, 52
Hall, William, 9n
Hamlet, 14n, 22, 24n, 81, 90
Harrison, John the Younger, 21, 44
Hart, Andreas, 44, 50n
Heawood, Edward, 75
Helme, John, 25
Henry IV, Part I, 22
Henry IV, Part II, 19, 27-37
Henry V, 40
Hill, Nicholas, 60
History of England, 20

History of Mervine, 25
History of the East and West Indies, 22
Hodgets, John, 22-3, 89
Hodgkins, John, 6
Honest Whore, 22-3, 87
How, William, 40, 43, 45, 50-1, 53, 61-4
Hymenaei, 23

In the time of Gods visitation, 109
Insatiate Countess, 100
Isaac, Col. Frank, 60, 86n

Jack Drums entertainment, 27
Jackson, Ralph, 14
Jackson, W. A., 9n, 10n
Jeffes, Abel, 45, 51, 64
Jenkins, Gladys, 88n
Jones, Richard, 6n
Judson, Thomas, 51-2, 60, 62, 86

Kingston, Felix, 25, 44, 60
Knight, Clement, 16, 20-1

Laura, 92
Law, Matthew, 18, 22-3
Leake, William, 23, 44
Legett, John, 44
Lemon, Robert, 109
Ling, Nicholas, 5, 12, 14, 16, 18-21, 23-6, 43, 80
Lockie, D. McN., 9n
Lownes, Humphrey, 14-5
Lownes, Matthew, 23-4

Macham, Samuel, 24
Malcontent, 22-3, 88, 94-101
Man, Thomas, 22
Matilda, 12, 14, 90
McKerrow, R. B., 12, 21, 43-5, 53, 83
McKerrow, R. B. and F. S. Ferguson, 43, 45, 53
Menaphon, 18
Meynell, Francis, 53
Miller, C. William, 50-2, 60, 62-4
Millington, Thomas, 19, 21
Mirror of martyrs, 20
Mœoniæ, 89-90
Monarchick tragedies, 22, 24
Morison, Stanley, 53
Morrison, Paul G., 5n, 12n, 21
Much ado about nothing, 19, 27-37
Mutton, Edmund, 21
Nashes lenten stuffe, 8n, 18, 86
New . . . defence of tobacco, 20

Newman, Widow, 12
Norton, Bonham, 16
Norton, Felix, 20
Norton, John, 64

Okes, Nicholas, 63
Old Fortunatus, 27n
Orwin, Thomas, 44
Oven, Henry, 9
Oxenbridge, John, 16-7, 43

Palladis Tamia, 60
Panegyric Congratulatory, 21
Paradoxes against common opinions, 20
Passions of the mind, 20, 22, 87
Pattern of painful adventures, 12, 81
Pavier, Thomas, 18, 20
Percy, *Lady* Lucy, 93
Pierce, W., 86n
Poems (Drayton), 23
Poetical rhapsody, 21
Poesy of floured prayers, 24, 91
Purfoot, Thomas, 24, 89

Queen Elizabeths tears, 24
Queen of Navarres tale, 16

Ratseys ghost, 89
Remains of a greater work, 88
Reynes, John, 60
Richard Duke of York, 19
Richard II, 16, 17, 79
Richard III, 16, 40-1, 86n
Roberts, James, 7, 14, 61, 89, 90
Rockit, Henry, 24
Rosalynde, 17
Royal Entertainment, 22-3

St. Peters complaint, 89-90
Schilders, R., 44
School of policy, 88
School of slovenrie, 82
Serle, Richard, 43
Sermons (Latimer), 8, 11, 15, 79
Seton, Gregory, 12, 43
Seven dialogues (Erasmus), 23, 94
Seven sinners, 24
Shapiro, I. A., 78n
Shawe, James, 21
Shoemakers Holiday, 9, 19, 25, 27-37, 81
Short, Peter, 44, 60
Short treatise of . . . penance, 17
Silkworms and their flies, 18
Simon, Oliver, 81n

Simmes, Richard, 5
Simmes, Valentine, *passim*
Simpson, Percy, 93-4
Singular salve, 109
Sir John Oldcastle, 18, 79
Smethwick, John 24
Solemn passion, 17
Song of Songs, 94
Sophonsiba, 89
Spencer, Hazleton, 101
Stafford, Simon, 17, 51
Stannary Laws of Devon, 8
Stevenson, Allan H., 64
Supplication of certain masspriests, 88
Survey of the popes supremacy, 14n
Sutton, Henry, 5
Sutton, Johane, 5

Table of good counsell, 109
Taming of a shrew, 24
Taylor, K. T., 45
Third proceeding, 15
Thomlyn, Arthur, 6
Thorpe, Thomas, 23, 94
Tofte, Robert, 93-4
Traitors . . . at Winchester, 8, 109
Treatise of . . . real presence, 15
Treatise of specters, 89

Trial of true friendship, 91
Triumphs over death, 16
Trognesius, Ioachim, 16
Troublesome raign of King John, 25
Trundle, John, 89
Truth and falshood, 14n, 15n
Two angry women, 27

Waldegrave, Robert, 44
Walker, Alice, 34
Warning of fair women, 18
Waterson, Simon, 19-20, 88
Weepe with ioy, 109
Welshbate, 8
What you will, 100
White, Edward Sr., 21, 24, 44
White, William, 6n, 19
Whitgift, *Archbishop*, 7, 18
Wilson, William, 61
Windet, John, 44, 89
Wise, Andrew, 16-7, 19, 25
Wolfe, John, 44
Wood, William, 20, 44
World of Wonders, 51
Works (Daniel), 19
Wright, John, 9, 10, 19
Wyllie, John Cook, 17n, 24n, 50n